T0209358

UNCONQUERED

Heart

*Overcoming Extraordinary Adversity and
Discovering Your True Purpose Through Faith*

KAT COOPER

WESTBOW
PRESS®
A DIVISION OF THOMAS NELSON
& ZONDERVAN

WestBow Press books may be ordered through booksellers or by contacting:

WestBow Press
A Division of Thomas Nelson & Zondervan
1663 Liberty Drive
Bloomington, IN 47403
www.westbowpress.com
844-714-3454

ISBN: 979-8-3850-0581-9 (sc)
ISBN: 979-8-3850-0582-6 (hc)
ISBN: 979-8-3850-0583-3 (e)

Library of Congress Control Number: 2023915990

Print information available on the last page.

WestBow Press rev. date: 09/26/2023

To my husband, Fred

In pondering my task to dedicate this work, such as it is, to the man who has been my rock, my friend, my comrade, and whom I am honored to call my spouse these twenty years, the words, Thank you, my Sweet Man, strike me as jejune; a repeat of the common-place expression uttered by me thousands of times throughout our lives together. As is the case of true love, the greatest gift from our Creator, we are left in awe, speechless. A writer who has lost her words is stymied and legless, having no volition.

In the presence of my silent desolation, I turn to the 18th-century poet Anne Bradstreet, who loved her mate as I love mine and who said it better than I ever could:

To My Dear and Loving Husband

If ever two were one, then surely we.
If ever man were lov'd by wife, then thee.
If ever wife was happy in a man,
compare with me, ye women, if you can.
I prize thy love more than whole Mines of gold,
Or all the riches that the East doth hold.
My love is such that Rivers cannot quench,
Nor ought but love from thee give recompence.
Thy love is such I can no way repay;
The heavens reward thee manifold I pray.
Then while we live, in love let's so persevere,
That when we live no more, we may live ever.

CONTENTS

FOREWORD

All happy families are alike; each unhappy family is unhappy in its own way.

-Leo Tolstoy, *Anna Karenina*

When I first read Leo Tolstoy's famous quote about families, I was struck not only by how succinctly he summed up family experience but also by the pathos inherent in his poignant observation. This reflection speaks of someone who has known suffering and disappointment.

It is the courage of the few, suffering in pain, broken by circumstance, who decide to lift your face upward and make the arduous journey out of the depths of despair towards the light. The path is steep; along the way, you encounter more difficulty than you anticipated or prepared for. Although the journey contains many moments of delight and joy, animated by the family you are part of and the friends you will make along the the way, many times, the decision feels like a mistake. You worry that following the path may be a more significant error in judgment than what landed you alone, sorrowful, and hurt.

At one point, the trail leads through a dark forest, obscuring the light. Feeling unsure of the way forward, you ask for help from the Paraclete. The Holy Spirit reminds you that He gifted you with all you need to reach your goal: faith, hope, charity, prudence, justice, temperance, and fortitude. The Lord endowed you with these virtues to sustain your quest as you enter the dark forest. Believing in that which we cannot see summons all the courage you possess and will provide the fortitude necessary to continue on your chosen journey.

Climbing a little higher, away from what has obscured your view, the light brightens your path forward as it becomes steeper and more difficult. Yet the trusty light illuminates every ledge and foothold, and you realize the pathway was not born of chaotic happenstance but created, *intended*. *You are supposed to walk this way.* Further up the path, the light reveals a cave. You stoop to enter and find a cleared area, a small pit dug out with logs and storage cases stacked by the walls. A large water tank stands like a sentinel near blankets, bedding, and a kettle. Somebody provided everything needed to continue on this journey. Someone knew we were coming and prepared a place for us. You are not alone. You are loved.

The following day, you awake refreshed and happy. Tendrils of light inch their way into the cave, and as you look out, you see it peeping over the far-off mountain tops, signaling the sun's morning ascent to the skies. You pack up your new provisions and leave the hospitable cave, joyful and excited to continue your journey. The morning sun shines brightly on the trail the Lord created for you. Although challenging, you trust the Lord that it will not be more arduous than you can bear. You know what you must do.

As you read this book, you will realize that, although you may not share my exact experiences, we share our humanity, the common denominator, as children of the Most High. Each of us will undergo our crucifixion, wait broken in the darkness, trusting that the morning and resurrection will surely come. There is no victory without defeat; there is no love without suffering.

Made in His image, the Lord called us forth to live this earthly life, and one day, He will call for us to return to Him. The Father sends us here to discover and fulfill our purpose for His glory. Our purpose in Him gives meaning to every experience we will have in this life, whether we choose to follow it or not. Taking the path of purpose that the Lord created for you will take great courage. But you are not alone.

You are not isolated. Your loving Father will provide all you need for the journey, for you are loved.

This book is a story of the Lord's victory in my life. It is a triumphant story of faith in the one true God.

A photo of my parents during the early years of their marriage

Chapter 1

THE FALL

Always pray to have eyes that see the best in people,
a heart that forgives the worst, a mind that forgets
the bad, and a soul that never loses faith in God.

ZSAZSA BELAGIO, ARTIST

Upon first glance, no two people seemed a more unlikely pair than Daddy and Mama. Mama's antecedents settled in Virginia before the Mayflower, joining a handful of other settlers hailed as the first families of Virginia. The other side of her family tree arrived in the New World on the Mayflower. They composed the ancestral line of younger siblings, including John Hancock's brother, affording Mama a patrician lineage, if not the grand estate, to accompany it.

Mama was delicate, porcelain-skinned, with red hair and blue eyes. I grew up witnessing the effect she had on those she met. Lovely and ladylike, she invariably left the impression of someone beautiful and genteel. Yet, Mama exuded a marked, almost eerie self-possession, an outlander moving through the world detached and entirely alone. The only child of older parents, her mother, my beloved Grammy, married Grandpa Ray, a man ten years older than her, at age 18, yet delayed pregnancy until her early 30s. Shortly after my mother's birth, Grammy suffered from 'women's problems and underwent a complete hysterectomy. As a result, the little family moved nearer to Grammy's parents, my great-grandparents, in Denver, Colorado so the family could be closer together.

Despite their happiness with their baby girl, Grandpa Ray's heavy drinking progressed into severe alcoholism. Eventually, their quiet tiny home became turbulent and explosive.

Unfortunately for my mother and the following generations of our family, as the inevitable alienation between the arguing spouses persisted, Grandpa Ray, an alcoholic prone to depression and low self-esteem, turned to his eight-year-old daughter for solace. Mama was mysterious in retelling this story, reluctant to provide any substantive details except to affirm that she was 'molested' by her father and to relate her mother's immediate, unequivocally decisive reaction. Upon finding out what had transpired between father and daughter, she ordered him out of the house until she could pack up herself and her little girl, leaving almost immediately for her mother's home. Grammy wasted no time in relating the details of her sudden departure from the marital home to her family. Given her family's ethos of silence around family troubles, Grammy's insistence upon legal separation and filing for divorce was almost unheard of in the beleaguered depression-era Mid-West of 1940. My grandmother remained silent about these events, even years later, after she realized what had happened to me. In response to my inquiries, I received the message loud and clear from my mother and grandmother: 'Let sleeping dogs lie.'

After decamping from her marital home, Grammy spent her days helping her mother feed the lines of starving men waiting at their back door for a bowl of soup. A year later, Japan bombed Pearl Harbor, and suddenly there were jobs and opportunities for both men and women. After several weeks of trying to secure employment in Denver, it became apparent that there were better-paying jobs out west in California's factories, shipyards, and airplane fabrication plants. Grammy, ever fearless and invincible, left my mother in the care of her parents and, with her 18-year-old niece in tow, traveled to the Bay Area of California and worked as a Rosie Riveter. The distance allowed the issues around the marital rupture, still never spoken of even after the divorce proceedings, to die down. In the ensuing months, my mother grew very close to her grandmother. They remained devoted to one another all of their lives.

After years of absence, broken only a few times by long train rides and brief visits to Denver, Mama finally joined her mother in Sacramento, where Grammy had moved with her new husband. My grandmother had married a widower with two older children, creating a blended family. Over time, Mama became fond of her much older siblings. However, her relationship with her new stepfather, my Grandpa Joe, was chilly. They all lived together in a large Victorian home until the older children moved out. In high school, Mama joined a conservative Baptist church near her home. After graduation, she left for Los Angeles at age 18 to attend their recommended institution, Biola College. She would meet my father during her senior year.

Dark-skinned with a rakish shock of thick, black hair, attesting to his Native American heritage, Daddy was nothing like the pale-faced, blue-eyed Protestant, all-American boys Mama encountered at school: Daddy had dark amber skin and deep brown eyes that could look right through you and seemed to want to. Born in Richmond, California, a poverty-stricken, crime-infested suburb of San Francisco, to a drug addict mother hooked on pain pills, his father never married his mother. He left the home long before his son was born. My paternal grandmother had five children that I knew of, four boys and a girl. Given that, at least three children were from different fathers and not always married to their mother, the family's home life could not have been more challenging.

At approximately ten years old, Daddy, the youngest sibling, was in grammar school and playing stickball in the street when a bakery truck struck and almost killed him. As Mama related the story to me, the truck did not halt but sped up, running over the little boy and crushing his legs and feet. The driver left as the little boy lay in the street, bleeding profusely. His oldest brother Dan, who witnessed the accident, carried him to the hospital, where the doctors saved his life. The medical team used many metal pins for his badly broken legs, and a large portion of both feet had to be amputated. His brothers and sister did their best to care for him when he returned home. However, his recovery was slow, and his movements were limited. He could no longer run and play with the other kids. The use of physical therapy to assist him wasn't sought by or offered to the family, so the range of motion in Daddy's lower extremities remained limited his entire life. Reportedly, his mother, indifferent to him before the accident, never visited the hospital and ignored him when he arrived home, limiting her interaction with him to a brief hello as she stole a pain pill from his prescription. The accident, his mother's response, and the shame he felt over his mangled legs and feet left indelible marks on that little boy. Embarrassed at his unsightly wounds, my father never wore shorts, even in the hottest summer months in Southern California. And he never let my sister and I see his disfigurement. These behaviors speak to his profound shame, humiliation, sadness, and isolation. The physical and emotional wounds my father endured as a child were deep and would cripple him emotionally.

As time passed, my father's home life continued haphazardly. Each child, preoccupied with their daily survival, found ways to cope: Daddy's oldest brother pursued his education; my father, the youngest sibling, left school without graduating and joined a gang. The untimely death of their beloved sister due to an illness neglected by their mother seems to have been the last straw for both my father and his oldest brother Dan: they left Richmond for Los Angeles, where Dan entered college, and my father joined the merchant marines.

Somewhere in his early 20s, Daddy formed a relationship with a young Hispanic woman, and they had a little boy. I have seen a picture of him as a toddler. The circumstances of their split and why my father was not a part of his son's life, I do not know.

On a lovely spring day in 1954, my father tried to call someone from a phone booth; he misdialed and reached my mother, a part-time receptionist for a legal firm in downtown Los Angeles. The last time I spoke to my father, he recounted the day he heard her voice on the phone. Enchanted, he kept her talking until she had to hang up. Finally, he was determined to meet her. That afternoon, he crossed town on public transport, located the office, and stood in the street watching her through a large picture window. He called again. Every time she had to hang up, he called back. He kept at it for a few days until she agreed to meet him for coffee.

My parents married after just a few months of dating. Mama left college, and they moved into a tiny house in the Boyle Heights neighborhood bordering East Los Angeles, a quiet enclave of immigrant families. Soon the romantic rush of love became disillusionment and disappointment. Mama realized early on that she had made a terrible mistake and wanted to leave. Pregnant soon after the wedding, she dreaded the future.

Much to Mama's regret, I was born the following summer at Lincoln Memorial Hospital, located nearby, which became a dorm for the University of Southern California in the future. In a Los Angeles County medical facility in the 1950s, delivery wards were large and not well-staffed. As a result, Mama suffered extreme labor pains and ruptured a blood vessel. By the time the staff found her, Mama had passed out, and the blood had seeped through the mattress and pooled under the bed. The team discovered my mother unconscious, her bed soaked in blood. She later told me she could see herself walking along the seashore and wading into the warm ocean up to her waist, something she was usually deathly afraid of, and working her way towards a long pier ahead of her. Mama said she knew she would be alright if she made it to the dock. Walking towards the pier, she remembered feeling calm and assured, as though she knew she would make it. However, just yards before the pier, she woke up in her hospital bed, nurses and doctors peering at her, very concerned. As Mama awoke, she realized she was in a different bed with fresh linens and a new nightgown. She started to cry. She had wanted it all to be over.

Unfortunately, her sadness moved from self-pity to profound depression when she met me. Thirty days premature, with thick hair and a pretty mouth, my left eye crossed inward; clearly, I could not see in that eye. The doctor explained that I was legally blind because of a congenital disability that had shut off the messages to the part of my brain that governed the left side. Thanks to medical advances, we now understand and can treat amblyopia effectively. My oldest grandson inherited the same syndrome; however, therapists trained his brain to access the eye by employing the current thinking in treatment and exercise. These practices also helped his eye to track with the other. These measures saved my grandson's sight, corrected his appearance, and he now sees normally. When I was five, medical science first implemented these advances on young children, and the doctors offered a plan to my parents to utilize these new techniques.

My parents enrolled me in the weekly program, necessitating a drive once per week to downtown Los Angeles. However, the unfortunate truth - that the problem with my sight lay in a congenital disability - left a lasting impression on my parents. Mama made the trip twice and then gave up. She later admitted that 'driving all the way downtown was too much trouble.' The sight in my left eye worsened; over time, the optic nerve atrophied, the left eye recrossed, and I lost my sight permanently. Later, when I suffered profound speech problems, they assumed the defect in my brain was far worse than initially diagnosed. Overwhelmed by the burden of my worsening medical condition, their aggravating financial circumstances, and marital unhappiness, Mama despaired of ever being able to leave Daddy.

Retelling my parent's first meeting sounds romantic, although nowadays, we think of him as stalking my mother. After studying family dynamics documented in childhood abuse studies, I consider my parent's marriage a coupling of two deeply wounded people who married their *"unconscious image of familiar love."* Mama suffered as a victim of childhood sexual abuse and feelings of abandonment because of her mother's long absences. Her family did not adequately address these ordeals. Mama never healed from these distressing experiences and unconsciously selected a man who would rewound her in similar ways. Profoundly wounded by an abusive mother who cast him aside, leaving him hurt, mutilated, and humiliated by her negligence, Daddy relived his youthful trauma of abandonment, triggered by Mama's desire to leave him soon after they wed.

***

And it used to be that when the Israelites had completed their sowing, Midian, Amalek, and the Kedemites would come up, encamp opposite them, and destroy the produce of the land and as far as the outskirts of Gaza, leaving no sustenance in Israel, nor sheep oxen or asses....Thus was Israel reduced to misery by Midian, and so the Israelites cried out to the Lord. [Judges 6:3-6 NAB].

The pillage and subjugation inflicted upon the Israelites in this chapter of Judges are relatable to almost everyone who reads it: we have all experienced the desolation of having high hopes as we work hard over time to achieve something; experience the joy and celebration of completing an arduous task, only to have your dreams dashed as you witness your accomplishment reduced to ashes.

Fortitude requires the nourishment of faith, hope, and dreams to stay the course of a cherished goal. As Mama later related the story of her marriage to me, despite her misgivings, she harbored secret hopes that the birth of a child would transform her marriage. Or, at the very least, allow her time at home to prepare to return to her mother's house with the baby in tow. But, as she rested in her hospital bed, events of the last year kept replaying in her mind: she married the wrong man and became pregnant; in planning her escape, she almost died from the delivery. And when she came to, the doctor informed her I was born with a congenital disability: a blind left eye that crossed. So, Mama commented later, ' I was stuck with your father and a half-blind baby.'

In the mid-1950s, the general opinion regarding physical anomalies was quite different than now. As a result, there was very little encouragement to pursue treatment. In Mama's mind, my apparent difficulties heralded a diminished future for both of us. Faced with realizing that her choices had authored her circumstances, Mama admitted she felt she was 'being punished.' Already carrying the heavy burden of childhood trauma, the shame and guilt associated with molestation, she now isolated from friends at church and became more depressed. To say she felt tied to a ponderous yoke is an understatement.

Twenty-three years later, I, too, suffered the same hopeless feelings as my mother. Thankfully, I had a therapist, attended Bible study at night, and went to church. I read the Gospels. I sensed I was not alone. I left my husband and a loveless and destructive marriage, taking my baby daughter with me. Initially furious and vindictive, he and I ultimately forged a partnership and raised our daughter in relative peace.

Over the years, I have turned countless times to this familiar passage in Matthew that quotes Jesus offering to ease the burdens of the afflicted:

> *Take my yoke upon you and learn from me, for I am*
> *meek and humble of heart, and you will find rest for*
> *your souls. For my yoke is easy, and my burden light.*
> [Matt 11:28-30 NCB]

Jesus' comforting words do not offer a cessation of trouble in this life; after spending time here on Earth as a human being, he is well aware of

7

our daily suffering. In this passage, Jesus acknowledges that our choices may make our burdens heavier. Most of us carry these afflictions alone; we do not expect others to assist us.

A yoke in the first century Judea was a piece of farm equipment that equally displaced the weight of a heavy load between two oxen. No animal or human can bear the weight of two yokes: the burden forces us to relinquish our yoke to assume this new easier yoke. In this exchange, Jesus, the Son of God, and God Himself, decidedly not human, lift the weight of our entire burden off our shoulders. As his beloved children, God did not mean for us to walk the earth without help, although He recognizes that in our rebellion, we often choose to do so. His active participation in our daily lives perfectly reflects God's Mercy by assuming the weight of our troubles and helping us to carry what we cannot bear alone.

Gideon is the hero of the story from Judges noted above. A younger sibling of the poorest family in Manasseh, Gideon's family came from a region of central Palestine named after the tribe of the same name that bordered both sides of the Jordan River. Many of the men in his family considered our hero too young and ineffectual to help overcome their oppressors, yet Gideon defeats the Midians. Initially reluctant to believe that God is speaking to him, Gideon asks the Lord for proof of who He is, which the Lord benevolently provides. *The Lord provided the help Gideon needed to grow in faith.* His faith affirmed Gideon turned to God for help in overcoming their enemies and received it.

Why do we hesitate to imitate Gideon and ask God to help us? In studying sacred scripture for several years, as well as participating in and leading Bible studies, I have observed that, when faced with life problems, believers fall into four groups whose response to problems in life seem to reflect their relationship with Jesus:

> Group #1 comprises those who have surrendered their lives to God and readily turn to Him for help in almost every situation.

> Group #2 includes believers who pray for the Lord's help and are obedient to His word until He provides the support needed, then promptly return to their old habits.

Group #3 contains the stubborn souls who believe in God and his saving power but abhor the sacrifice, discipline, and obedience required to obtain it. Members of Group #3 share an abiding belief in their competence, strength, and omnipotence, preferring to find a solution within themselves and in their way.

Finally, Group #4 contains the hapless souls suffering from shame and guilt over our past. This deep humiliation hinders their ability to reach out to Jesus for help. Often abandoned and abused, many people suffer profound disappointment and distrust in others for concrete reasons. Isolated and afraid, rejected and sad, Group #4 feels stuck - too fearful of staying as they are, too anxious to step forward.

Mama belongs to the fourth group. My mother grappled with feelings of shame her entire life. Rooted in her father's sexual abuse and her perceived abandonment by my grandmother, the discovery of Daddy's past exacerbated her inner turmoil.

Disappointment in others is a reliable vehicle to separate ourselves from Christ. No doubt, Daddy found in Mama his dream girl and misled her about his family, background, and relationships to avoid scaring her away. When revealed, the truth must have frightened a 22-year-old Baptist coed who did not wear makeup or dance with boys in adherence to her church's precepts. Despite what he saw as his honest efforts to make the marriage work, his lying was a hurtful betrayal for her. When the truth became known, some of him hoped it wouldn't matter. But it did. Daddy's hurt reverted to his anger as a teenage gang member; he became the illegitimate little boy from the streets whose mother didn't love him. The chasm between them grew wider. Mama, who had lived amongst the faithful, well versed in prayer yet harboring shame and guilt, turned away from the God she was sure was punishing her. With no spiritual training, Daddy attended church with Mama to please her and did not know where to begin, and Mama wasn't helping.

The saddest aspect of speculating about what might have been in this tragic story is how close they were to healing, redemption, and a new life. Jesus reaches for us in every moment. He comes closer to us. *The Lord meets us where we are.* As a divinity, Jesus has the power to speak healing and wholeness into each of us from a distance, yet he heals through connection. Our Lord touched the deaf mute. He healed the blind man and exorcised the boy oppressed by demons. The hands that embraced the leper willingly stretched out on the Cross, allowing nails to be driven into His hands to save us all from ourselves. Jesus knew my parents' sins and the terrible mistakes they would make several years later. And still, He reached for them as he reached for each of us.

Just like the woman who suffered for twelve years from vaginal hemorrhaging we read about in the Gospel of Mark [Mark 5:24-34 NASB], we hide away our shameful secrets. Afraid to admit her ailment, the woman preferred to reach for Jesus, secretly touch His garment, and experience the power of divine love heal her in an instant. Yet, Jesus instinctively understood that the cure required more than healing her physical ailment: He needed to extend that healing grace to her spiritual and emotional brokenness. In insisting upon meeting and speaking to her, Jesus acknowledges her directly, includes her, singles her out in his esteem, and affirms her extraordinary act of faith.

Perhaps Mama and Daddy made the same mistake many of us make: *we believe that voice in our heads that tell us we are too wretched a sinner to be redeemed.* Our embarrassment over sin and failure drive us into isolation. Jesus knows the depth of our wounds, immorality, and sorrows. The Son of Man experienced every temptation we face: He experienced being tempted but chose not to sin. St. Paul, a flawed man himself, encourages us to turn to Jesus when we are too ashamed to admit our guilt:

> 'Therefore, since we have a high priest who has passed through the heavens, Jesus, the Son of God, let us hold fast to our confession, for we have not a high priest who is unable to sympathize with our weaknesses but one who in every respect has been tempted as we are, yet without sin. Let us then confidently approach the throne with grace so we may receive mercy and find grace when we need help. Every high priest is taken from among men

to represent them in their dealings with God, to offer gifts and sacrifices for sins. He can deal patiently with ignorant and misguided people since He, too, is subject to weakness. And as a result of this, he must make sinful offerings for himself as well as for the people.' [Letter to the Hebrews 4:14-16; 5:1-3 NCB]

Jesus desires to redeem us all and return us to God. Yet we hesitate, afraid of a repeat of the betrayal and abandonment or, if we are honest, a bruised ego and the relinquishment of some of our less-than-holy habits. So we ignore the knock on the door; we hide from Him. We have developed a thousand ways to hide from God: career, family, friends, shopping, social media, working too much, and procrastination, to name just a few.

Working in alcohol rehab centers, I saw firsthand how difficult it was for many patients to accept that they had a problem. For others, the first time police arrest them for drunk driving or their spouse asks them to leave is sufficient motivation to admit they have a problem and seek help. The alcoholic or addict who continues their destructive behavior even after these deterrents usually has to "hit bottom ." As alcoholism is a progressive disease, the deterioration of body, mind, and soul becomes painfully apparent to everyone around them. Yet they would stubbornly refuse to admit they could not stop their compulsion to drink.

The antidote for the false pride that covers underlying shame: humility. Yet many of us feel too embarrassed to confide in a friend or to go to confession. In both instances, the fear of the friend or priest's negative opinion of them prevents them from seeking the help and grace they need. St. John Chrysostom advised, "Be ashamed when you sin, not when you repent."

St. Augustine of Hippo, Doctor of the Church, embodied the reluctant convert. Augustine pursued a life of pleasure and licentiousness throughout the years he spent pursuing advanced education in the waning years of the Roman Empire. His academic pursuits exposed him to various philosophies. For a brief period, he was a follower of the Gnostic movement, specifically the Manicheans, avoiding the Christianity that his long-suffering mother, St. Monica, had converted to. After completing his education, he lived with a woman he never married, fathered a child, and lived openly with her for years.

Reading the life of St. Anthony the Great and the account of St. Anthony's life of asceticism touched Augustine's heart and led to his ultimate conversion. St. Augustine recorded in his profoundly moving and relatable book, *Confessions*, the account of his confession to Jesus in the company of his friend Alypius: weeping, he flung himself down under a fig tree next to his friend, in despair over his sins and wanting desperately to change his life, he pleads with the Lord, How long O Lord, how long? At that moment, he overheard a chorus of people chanting from a house nearby *Pick it up! Please pick it up and read it!* Assuming this was divine intervention and the chanting referred to Holy Scripture, he picked up a copy with him and opened it to Romans. 'Let's behave properly as in the day, not in carousing and drunkenness, not in sexual promiscuity and debauchery, not in strife and jealousy. But put on the Lord Jesus Christ, and make no provision for the flesh in regard to its lusts.' [Romans 13:13-14 NASB] Reading further, St. Augustine found the grace of Jesus, "Accept the one whose faith is weak, without quarreling over disputable matters." [Romans 14:NIV] Reading this passage in Romans forever changed St. Augustine's life.

The moment of conversion is very personal: we feel our heart breaking as we contemplate our sins and mistakes, and it seems inconceivable that our life can move forward without a full confession. Others may sense a gradual awakening; knowledge that seemed to elude them is suddenly explicit: *this is the way to go, the step I should take.* The one universal aspect we all share: our spirit feels shattered under the weight of shame and regret. The need to cleanse our conscience and heal our souls is overwhelming.

Because the Lord creates us in His image, within our human beingness, although fallen, we retain a resemblance or facet of the goodness of God regardless of our transgressions. Sin is an anathema to that natural goodness. But because of our separation from God's presence and that we live in a fallen world, we often do not entirely grasp what sin is or the depth of the chaos we have created. As defined in the *Catechism of the Catholic Church, sin has a double consequence. Grave sin deprives us of communion with God. It, therefore, makes us incapable of eternal life, the deprivation of which is called "eternal punishment" of sin.*

On the other hand, every sin, even venial, entails an unhealthy attachment to creatures, which must be purified here on earth or after death in the

Purgatory state. This purification frees one from the "temporal punishment" of sin. We should not confuse these two punishments as a kind of vengeance inflicted by God from without but as a natural, inevitable consequence of sin. A conversion that proceeds from a fervent charity can attain the complete purification of the sinner in such a way that no punishment would remain.

This passage from the *Catechism of the Catholic Church* is vital: many of us who have suffered from the consequences of our sins feel very angry at God as though He is cruel to us. Our faith can be tested in these moments, especially if we are victims of someone else's sin. *However, it is not God doing it to us but the natural consequence of sinful choices.* The Lord gave us the precious gift of free will, and He will not obstruct that free will even if we make sinful choices or choose to harm another person. I remember lying in my bunk bed and asking aloud *why you let this happen to me.* I was too little to understand that my father might use the Lord's gift of free will for evil deeds. However, the same merciful God would later allow me to turn away from the darkness of my family and choose the light of Jesus.

What I also know to be true is that, yes, we are all saved by the Blood of Jesus and our faith in him. But that is not the end of the business. If our plan is to be baptized and then to assume, despite our subsequent actions and choices, that we are safe from damnation and thus resume our previous selfishness, why would Jesus call us to corporal works of mercy in, among others, the Great Commandments, the Beatitudes, and the Book of James? As an adult convert, I knew well that in the Sacrament of Baptism, the Lord's Grace cleansed me of all sin *until that moment*; what transpired after I left the church was something else altogether. Jesus, speaking to the adulterous woman at the well (no surprise that water was nearby!), who was so ashamed of her situation that she covered up her sin by referring to her current lover as her spouse after speaking of the promise of eternal life, said to her, 'Go on your way, and sin no more.'[The Gospel of John 8:11 NCB]

Baptism imparts new life by water, and the Spirit indelibly marks each of us for God as we become members of the Body of Christ. Baptism imparts sanctifying grace; we now share in God's life and receive the three theological virtues of faith, hope, and charity (love). The Cardinal virtues of wisdom or prudence, courage, temperance, and justice, placed in our hearts when we are born, known as *The Natural Law,* seem to fuse with the Theological virtues of faith, hope, and charity we received at baptism.

Baptism profoundly changes us in ways we might not have expected. Our spiritual status changes: as a new members of the Body of Christ, we ascend to the new positions of priest, prophet, and king. This elevation implies the responsibility of not only ourselves but to join with others of the Church to assist them as well, to live a good life, striving towards greater holiness and obedience to God's law and will.

The concept of membership in Jesus's church incurs a joining with our brothers is especially important because the salvation we seek is not just ours personally. God calls us to *share* in the life of our brothers and to *love* them, to *help* them, to give them one of our two shirts if need be. St. Paul succinctly states, "If one member suffers, all suffer together with it. If one member is honored, all rejoice together with it." [1 Corinthians 12:26 NCB] The same can be said of sin: when one of us sins, we are all affected. It is an erosion in the Body of Christ. In our modern culture, the lines between acceptable and unacceptable become blurry and indistinct; we cross them repeatedly without entirely comprehending the consequences of what we have done. Yet armed with the gifts of baptism, our conscience bolstered by grace, we recognize our mistakes; we *know* we have erred. Our eyes are open. We can never unknow the truth that now resides in our hearts. These needling pricks of your conscience are the Holy Spirit, sent by our merciful Lord, working to save your life and soul. Avail yourself of the sacraments. Whether you are Catholic or Protestant, Jew, Hindu or Moslem, no matter how long it has been since you attended your place of worship, make an appointment to confess your sin, and, if you are catholic, ask for absolution. Do not hesitate. Avail yourself of the salvation Jesus died for and reclaim your place as priest, prophet, and king.

Mama admitted her sins to me just before she died. She struggled to believe I had forgiven her. Finally, we experienced a moment together in which she knew I had forgiven her. As I held her hand and prayed, Mama died in peace. Although my mother's family members still deal with the effects of what transpired, I ensured my daughter's safety. The wheel of suffering that originated with my Grandfather Raymond's sinful incest continued to crush consecutive generations.

My maternal grandfather's sins had lasting ramifications that have affected three generations of my family. A palpable darkness had settled upon my family; Grammy never spoke of him again. And Mama harbored resentful feelings towards Grandpa Ray, refusing to talk to him or to answer any questions about her father until just before he died. The crimes my father perpetrated upon all of us sent my mother into a life-long shame spiral. Mama died having admitted that the incest occurred and admitting to additional occurrences she witnessed, confidences I had shared with her as young as four years old, as well as a well-baby visit on my six-month birthday at which the doctor inquired as to why my vagina appeared 'damaged,' my hymen broken. In every case, Mama continued blaming Daddy entirely for what happened. My mother never spoke of her collaboration in the 10-year cover-up of verbal, physical, and sexual abuse perpetrated by my father. Instead, she hushed up, covered over, and disregarded her responsibility to protect me.

My paternal grandmother essentially disowned Daddy; it is doubtful he was baptized as a baby or child, not an adult. My father never admitted the full extent of his crimes to anyone. It is difficult for me to contemplate Daddy's eternal fate. After I started attending church with Mama as a teenager, she told me much of the story. Experiencing the first glimpses of faith and communion with other believers helped me start the healing process. And with that healing came the recognition of the profound tragedy of my father's life. The sadness I feel for him is bottomless. He died unredeemed and afraid, separated from his wife, daughters, and the little boy he disowned over 70 years ago, just as his mother had abandoned him. I forgave my father years ago; I carry no animosity toward him. I pray for the souls of both my parents every day.

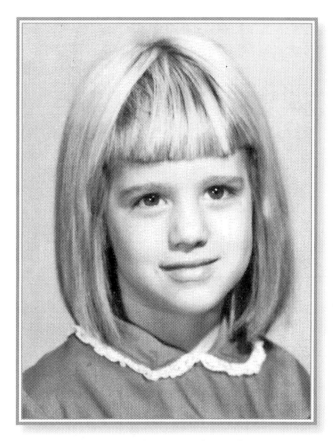

Me, aged five years, September 1960, after my first eye surgery, as kindergarten was starting, and the beginning of this story

Chapter 2

STONE

The tongue has the power of life and death, and
those who love it will eat its fruits.

FROM WHAT I LEARNED LATER, as a toddler, our family moved several times, returning to the east side of Los Angeles when I was almost five. We selected a small two-bedroom, one-bath duplex near the freeway on-ramps. East Los Angeles was the chosen destination for thousands of Black and Hispanic workers and their families seeking employment in the defense industry in what came to be known as the Second Great Migration of the 1940s. East Los Angeles of the 1960s was a rough-and-tumble district possessing the dubious distinction of being one of only two areas exempt from the racially restrictive city covenants—the infamous *redlining* - which prevented minorities from renting or purchasing property in other Southern California communities. Despite a 1948 court ruling deeming these practices illegal, and the subsequent passing of the Rumford Fair Housing Act, enacted to ease homeownership for minorities, change came slowly to post-war Southern California.

Our neighborhood was a slice of the American melting pot and included a variety of ethnic representations: Black, Hispanic, Asian, a sprinkling of Middle Eastern, and Caucasian. Living in East Los Angeles, our bi-racial family - Mama was White; Daddy was half Native American, half Caucasian rendering his skin a deep brown color and his hair jet black - we experienced less of the looks, sneers, and mumbling that often occurred when visiting downtown. However, we were still the exception, not the rule, as multi-racial families were not the norm.

These distinctions were more critical in the 1960s; people rarely intermarried, preferring to choose their partners from within their cultural group. Mama's red hair and blue eyes, as well as my waist-length blonde hair, seemed to shout WHITE! Whenever the whole family went grocery shopping at the Mercado. The sideways looks and mumbling would intensify whenever Daddy went with us. No one knew what to make of him. He was well aware of his impact on others: he would not glare back or seem to react. Neither he nor Mama acknowledged or answered the implied question behind the socially acceptable query, "How *did* you two *meet?*" I was always proud of them for that.

Our family was very close to our family doctor. He was a lovely and patient man, the only medical practice near us for years. The waiting room would be bursting with waiting patients every day of the work week, a line outside the door forming from very early in the morning until the last patient left after 6:00 pm. Yet he found time to see us if we stopped by, knowing that I had put on my new Easter clothes just for him, he would stop everything on a busy Good Friday afternoon to admire me and tell me how pretty I was. As my 5th birthday approached, this same dedicated, kind physician had been researching ways to help me with my blind left eye. White Memorial Hospital, a bit of a hike in traffic from our home in East Los Angeles, had started an experimental program for amblyopia in children. First, I would undergo surgery to shorten the eye muscles and realign the crossing of my left eye. Then, after recovery and a few days' rest, I would leave the hospital with a patch on my left eye. After my surgery healed, I would need to return weekly for at least six months to complete further treatment and hand-to-eye coordination exercises. Upon examination, the physicians at White Memorial felt confident that careful adherence to their regime would avoid the permanent diminishment of my sight. Additional benefits included strengthening the eye muscles, preventing my left eye from crossing again, and improving depth perception. My mother later admitted to me that the doctors at White Memorial were emphatic: adherence to this protocol was the only way to restore sight and prevent a very noticeable recrossing of my left eye. Now an accepted protocol for this congenital problem, it was a groundbreaking treatment in 1960. My parents enrolled me in the program, and I underwent surgery. As expected, I left the hospital three days later with a patch on my left eye.

However, after several weekly trips to White Memorial, Mama gave up on the program as it was 'too much trouble to drive to White Memorial.' We never returned to the program after I had healed from surgery and discarded the eye patch. And, as the doctors predicted, within months, my left eye crossed again. Subsequent yearly eye exams showed the optic nerve in my left eye had atrophied, and, except for colors, any gains in my eyesight disappeared.

A few months after my surgery and recovery, I heard the sound that would change my life. My family had retired for the night when a sound nearby startled me. The muffled noise was unmistakable in the close quarters of our tiny duplex. Lying in my bed, I could hear the bedroom doorknob turn, the hinges creak, and the heavy footsteps of my father's work boots enter the room. Alarmed, I lay still, hoping he would believe I was still sleeping and not disturb me. Daddy had a terrible temper; his recent outbursts scared all of us, especially my mother. Worried that I was in trouble again, I could feel my heart beating faster and faster, the back of my neck becoming moist. As he checked to see if I was asleep, he bent down to sit beside me. As I faced the wall, my father lay his hand on my left side. He gently shook me. I lay still. He shook me harder. I still did not respond. Daddy then lay on the bed beside me, slipped his hands under the covers, and molested me. I can remember silently praying *Jesus, take me away! Make me disappear!* My eyes filled with tears, *Jesus, take me now. Let me die.* Minutes later, tears streaming down my face, my father rolled over, sighed, and stood up, quietly leaving the room and returning to his bedroom and my sleeping mother.

My father's attentions would become infrequent nightly visits, repeating the same pattern. However, as I said nothing and Mama didn't confront him over time, Daddy became more emboldened, his nightly visits more frequent, especially as I turned six. This new birthday heralded the start of my latchkey existence as well. That September, I started first grade, and Daddy began working the day shift, returning at night at about the same time as Mama. At night Daddy's visits increased, and I became more and more introverted, afraid to tell Mama as I was sure she would be angry and blame me. In the morning, I was to walk to and from school, a key pinned to the inside of my dress. In my distress, I turned inward and stopped speaking at school. The kids would point at me and laugh. The nurse sent a note home pinned to my shirt in one incident. I cannot recall what I had done to prompt the nurse to write this note, but I do recall Mama's reaction: she read the message, glared at me, and threw it away. That evening I can remember even more tension between Daddy and Mama: she was sullen and standoffish to all of us; he was silent and sulking, not turning away from the newspaper even when Mama called us for supper. After dinner and the dishes, I escaped to my room to color and read my book. So began my commitment to silence.

In a therapy session, I invited my mother to later on as an adult, Mama confessed to being aware of what had occurred between my father and me, and, recalling the nurse's note, we realized this must have been the first time someone in authority noticed the signs of abuse. Later in that session, Mama cried and admitted Daddy molested me before I could walk. She recounted the story of a baby wellness exam when I was six months old that revealed an internal injury. The pediatrician confronted my mother, asking how this injury may have happened..? My mother admitted to me she shrugged her shoulders and did not reply. The upshot of that therapy session was her admission that my mother had known about most of the incidences when my father entered my bedroom, touched me, pulled me aside, and, specifically, each time he forced me to perform. *My mother knew and tacitly agreed.*

Unthinkable now, 60 years later and in the era of *Me-Too*, this well-baby-visit-inquiry-and-rebuff became the avoidance-of-reporting pattern when outsiders questioned the goings-on in our family home. Someone outside the family, a friend, teacher, or another authority figure, sends a note home, tries to call my mother at work, or asks her directly why I am bruised, cut, scratched, swollen, or bleeding somewhere. Momma ignores the notes; refuses the call; hangs up on the nurse; cries and begs the doctor not to alert the authorities; promises the school nurse that Daddy hit me 'just happened the one time'; or shrugs her shoulders, refusing to answer questions. The pattern continued until I was in high school.

When researching the behaviors of abusers, I learned that the perpetrators and their enablers could compartmentalize their destructive and neglectful behavior from their everyday life. This phenomenon played out in my family. My daytime father was outwardly distant, although occasionally affectionate. However, at night, unimpeded by my mother, he would enter my bedroom, seeking the solace he craved from his oldest daughter. Mama continued to pretend that nothing was happening.

In this therapy session, Mama and I could recall only one time when I went to her for help: I asked her if Daddy ever got mad at her when they were together. Mama responded with her usual silence. However, after this unanswered question, she confided her disgust with their marital life. It did not occur to Mama that her behavior was highly inappropriate, placing an excessive burden upon a six-year-old abused child. Mama maintained her restrained silence around others we knew, including family members. With me, she was more forthcoming. I stood there, silent, stunned, not comprehending some of what she said and not knowing how to respond. My reason for existence was to solace my parents in their marital unhappiness based on their needs. I felt like I was disappearing.

That same year, 1960, saw the election of John F. Kennedy to the presidency of the United States. Anticipation amongst the Black and Hispanic minorities in Central, South, and East Los Angeles districts ran high. However, President Kennedy did not press the civil rights agenda as hard as these communities would have preferred: JFK had identified several legislative goals he hoped to enact and required support from the Southern states to pass them. By appointing several Black Americans to key positions within his administration, JFK signaled his future intentions for the nation. Despite what some viewed as worrying harbingers of the reforms to come, relative peace seemed to settle in and around the *barrios* of Los Angeles.

By the following spring of 1961, President Kennedy, to support 1400 Cuban guerilla fighters determined to oust the Cuban Marxist, Fidel Castro, launched an offensive that failed miserably. Trained and outfitted by the CIA, the small band of warriors loyal to the previous Batista government was no match for Castro's army, surrendering within 24 hours—a humiliating black mark for the new Kennedy administration.

After the fateful spring of 1961 and President Kennedy's Bay of Pigs debacle, the fall of 1961 saw a deepening crisis in foreign affairs as relations between the Soviet Union and Cuba became normalized, and the U.S. relationship with these two countries deteriorated further. That I can recall these events so clearly speaks to the urgency of the crisis. President Kennedy and the rest of the world, including my parents, kept a watchful eye on the small island 90 miles south of Miami. In the early 1960s, television networks restricted news reports until 6:00 pm. During the Cuban Missile Crisis, we continued our Sunday strolls down Wilshire Boulevard to window shop. Daddy would buy us ice cream after lunch, and we would stand next to him as he and Mama stared at the news through the picture window at the T.V. store. Teachers would pull one another aside at school and discuss the newspapers at length. Preoccupied with what might happen, the principal ordered multiple emergency drills with teachers instructing us to hide under our desks, arms folded over our heads. I moved through the initial weeks of first grade with no one noticing my worsening speech.

This same speech faltering, which had begun as an occasional stutter before kindergarten, had now developed into a debilitating stammer. Daddy's visits to my bed continued, and I stopped talking by Christmas. At school, I would isolate myself. I didn't know how to relate to my peers. The weight of what I was experiencing at home silenced me. My crossed eye and clumsiness had already become a source of mean-spirited banter in the schoolyard. I remember feeling relieved when the kids began to avoid me: I was worried that if I had made friends, they would want to come over and play in my room. What would I do? Suppose Daddy was angry, or Mama threw the frying pan at Daddy again? Anything could happen and often did. Fearful that I might accidentally reveal the conditions of my home life, I avoided everyone, sat under a tree, read books, and daydreamed.

I gave up; my spirit seemed to collapse within itself. By third grade, my silence was so pervasive both my parents became convinced that the doctors had missed something in my original diagnosis and that, in actuality, I *was* defective. Moreover, hearing the two of them discuss my lack of verbalization and interaction with others convinced me that whatever was wrong with me was far worse than the doctors had led them to believe. At one point, my parents discussed what they thought were my limited options in life, as though I wasn't there or unable to comprehend.

Their best-case scenario: is that someone would deign to marry me after high school if I graduated.

Shortly after this fateful conversation, Mama, frustrated with what she perceived as my lack of innate intelligence, was 'as slow-witted as a stone.' Later, as the entire phrase became too cumbersome for the shorthand of family life, she abbreviated this moniker to what became her favorite nickname for me: 'stone .' Even after I graduated from nursing school and later earned a bachelor of science degree, these achievements did not convince Mama that I possessed sufficient intelligence, talent, or ability to make anything of my life. Nevertheless, Mama used this nickname well into my adulthood.

My immediate family failed to recognize that congenital blindness, diminished hand-to-eye coordination, a lack of depth perception, severe speech impediment, the effects of sexual abuse, and the weight of shame and humiliation had left me emotionally exhausted. My outward countenance must have appeared mystifyingly opaque. By my eighth birthday, they assumed their blind, stuttering, downcast daughter possessed yet another organic problem and that there was no hope for me.

During this early period, much time was spent hiding in corners and closets, burying my face in the books and encyclopedias Daddy purchased, and crying quietly alone. We had adopted a Tabby cat, and Mama named Mickey. I liked to hold him close and talk to him. Amiable and compliant, the enormous orange cat would sit with me for quite a while before asking to leave. But, of course, I didn't pour out my heart to even this genial, furry friend: no words were spoken, even when I was alone. But within the snug confines of the messy clothes closet or lying on my bunk bed was a measure of safety and respite from the turmoil down the hall.

Two years later, it was 1962, and the nation celebrated the successful end of the Cuban Missile Crisis. The military provided news services with black and white photos taken from a plane of the site where the missiles were first spotted, now removed. The sense of impending doom had lifted. Neighbors had gathered on the large communal lawns out front to talk and laugh; my parents did not join the fun but were thrilled. As the hazy sun descended, I watched the happy celebration of our neighborhood outside from our front stoop. I then peered inside at my parents, who were chatting and smiling. To join them seemed too far to go. By then,

Daddy had become a regular nighttime visitor, and Mama continued to confide her troubles to me; my continuing silence had convinced both of my parents that my mental impairment was permanent. The nickname 'stone' - implying what my intelligence was equal to - was used regularly. My family, neighborhood, and schoolmates kept their distance; my isolation was complete.

Born blind in one eye, with dwarfism and severe curvature of the spine in 1287 to a family of the minor nobility living in Perugia, Saint Margaret of Castello's parents were ashamed of their baby daughter and hid her from view. A household maid took pity on her, named her Margaret, and kept her fed and warm for six years. Finally, despite the intense secrecy of her existence, the parents, worried about public opinion, moved the little girl to a prison cell where she was to remain at all times except to attend Mass and receive the sacraments. The family chaplain was allowed to instruct her in the faith, but she was not allowed any visitors. At one point, her father, still concerned about detection, spoke to a mason working at the castle and requested that he seal the cell up: her father intended to leave her there until her death.

We can never fully appreciate the harrowing that must have been for a small child, having already experienced her parent's rejection and being entirely dependent upon the kindness of servants. Fortunately, the imminent threat of a surprise invasion stymied her father's gruesome plan. Clothed in black, little Margaret and her mother escaped to the family's other castle at Mercatello, where somebody locked the little girl in a cell under similar conditions. Those servants aware of the little girl's plight were heartsick for her and showed her small kindnesses secretly, worried her father might find out. Margaret's living conditions continued this way until 1303, when her mother suggested they take the little girl to a nearby Franciscan church famous for its healing miracles. Unfortunately, the little girl was not healed. Her father lost his patience and ordered the servants to leave her at the church when they left.

Initially a beggar, little Margaret slept with the other homeless people outside near the church. The low-income families attending Mass there often saw her walking the grounds, her tiny, limping body familiar to the townspeople. Many found her praying in the back of the church every day for hours. When approached, Margaret would smile and ask about the children or family of the inquirer. Margaret became known for her kindness to other homeless people, and some families offered to foster her, rotating the child and her care from family to family. As Margaret grew older, she assisted the low-income families who helped prisoners and other poor, homeless people. Nicknamed "Metola," after her parent's castle, she opened a school for the children of the poor. The nuns at a nearby convent offered her a place in their community; however, this placement was short-lived as the nuns had little patience with her physical limitations, and Metola, evidencing solid piety, wasn't comfortable with the nun's slapdash approach to the convent life. The nuns and Metola parted ways, and she returned to her foster parents. Familiar with the Dominican friars newly established in her town, they later admitted her to the Third Order of Saint Dominic and received her. Margaret adopted the clothing of a cloistered religious and wore her habit until her death on April 12, 1320. Vast crowds attended her funeral and, upon seeing the outdoor burial spot selected for her by the parish priest, demanded that her remains be interred within the church. The priest initially refused until he witnessed the healing of another disabled girl at the funeral. Finally, he relented, and they buried her inside the church.

Over hundreds of years, one pope beatified Margaret, and she later received additional recognition from two others. Finally, Pope Francis opted to forgo the usual last steps to sainthood and declared Margaret of Castello, a saint on April 24, 2021. Her feast day is April 13.

I learned from this story that the retelling, documentation, and subsequent beatification of this martyred child speaks to what we all knew and may not realize: history is littered with the tales of abandoned, abused children, some recognized, most long forgotten. Although then as now, many of the abused, neglected children turn to theft or other crimes in an attempt to salvage some existence, Margaret of Castello's story highlights the path many mistreated children do not choose: a way of hope, faith and an openness to the kindness of others. This openness to the charity of strangers is what I believe preserved Margaret's inherent charity, the very virtue the Lord places in all of our hearts, for we are created in His Image.

For many adult children of abusive homes, the hurt and anger from years of mistreatment create a kind of hardened crust around their hearts, and they turn to what they learned: sin. Feeling justified in their behavior for sins committed against them, they pursue a life of degradation, turning away from the light that seeks them in their darkness. In the parable of the Prodigal Son, the Apostle Luke recounts the story, noting in the narrative that, upon the prodigal son's return, although still far off, as his father glimpsed him in the distance, he 'was filled with compassion for him; he ran to his son, threw his arms around him and kissed him.' [Luke 15:20 NIV] The hiking up his robes to run down the lane some distance to greet his wayward son, clasp him tight and kiss him in public is not typical for a first-century wealthy patriarch. A man of that stature would behave almost ceremoniously in public; others would approach *him*, even his wife and family. *It is the unabashed love and acceptance of his father that heals his son's wounded heart.* The prodigal son's bodily hunger may have driven him to seek his family home, but his father's profound demonstration of love and forgiveness is what kept him there. *The light seeks us even in our darkness.*

It may surprise many that another child not especially wanted by his father was the hero of the Jewish people: David, the great king. In studying the life of David, the illustrious antecedent of Jesus, we learn that not only did his father initially fail to acknowledge him or even to present him to the prophet Elijah when the prophet asked to meet his sons, David's following father figure, King Saul, who loved the boy, grateful to him for slaying Goliath, would later become jealous of David's success and attempt to kill him. In Psalm 34, we read David's sad sigh of relief and gratitude to God for his deliverance from his betrayer, the very same father figure, King Saul:

> The righteous person may have many troubles,
> but the Lord delivers him from them all;
> He protects all of his bones,
> not one of them will be broken.

Evil will slay the wicked;
the foes of the righteous will be condemned.
The Lord will rescue his servants;
no one who takes refuge in him will be condemned.
[Psalm 34:19-22 NIV}

Modern translations of Psalm 34, verse 19 from the original Hebrew, reveal David's choice of the word *shavar* to describe the depth of his hurt at the treachery of Saul and speaks of his profound pain. The American Standard Bible translation is poignant: The Lord is close to the brokenhearted and saves those whose spirit is crushed. [Psalms 34:18 NIV]

After years of therapy, prayer, workshops, group counseling, retreats, studying scripture, and receiving spiritual direction, I met many people who shared this same hurt over a parental betrayal. I realized that Daddy's abusive behavior was not only monstrous; he was also emotionally, spiritually, and physically broken. My therapist suggested he was probably sociopathic: Daddy did not register guilt for his crimes. His brokenness had robbed him of his humanity and connection to God.

Yet it was not Daddy's terrible abuse that cut the deepest: it was my mother's betrayal and refusal to protect me and to reject and punish me when I asked for help. Mama, who, for years, was angry with my father over their marital issues, allowed him to abuse and molest me physically. In addition, she masterminded the cover-up of Daddy's heinous crimes. My mother's duplicity inflicted the most long-lasting damage upon my heart and soul.

Many of us carry a cross of betrayal at the hands of a family member, friend, or coworker. Initially shocked and disbelieving, we retrace the steps that led to the event, asking ourselves, *What did I do?* We think that if we understand whatever mistake we make, the actual behavior of this person will somehow feel less hurtful. Later, someone will ask you if you have seen so-and-so recently, and you reply no, to which they press the inquiry still further, *Why? Were you two such good friends?* To explain would require retelling what transpired, yet even touching that precious hurt pocket of the heart is too scary for most of us. We mumble something unintelligible, change the subject, and try to bury that painful experience and move on. After this regrettable reminder of our recent loss, we lie in our beds, not sleeping, unable to erase in our minds what lies underneath the persistent question of what we did to deserve to be treated this way.

David, chosen by God to rule over the nations of Israel and Judah and to establish a royal lineage that would one day produce the Messiah, was also not the favored child of his father. God instructed the prophet Samuel to locate Jesse's son, anoint him with the holy oil, and pronounce him king. Samuel concerned that he would select the wrong young man, asked the Lord to make his choice known. The Lord was clear that the holy oil would flow over only the chosen son and no other. Samuel asked to see Jesse's sons, bringing forth his oldest three: Eliab, Abinadab, and Shammah. But when Samuel attempted to anoint the boys, the oil would not flow. He asked if there were any other sons, and regretfully, Jesse sent for the youngest son, David. For him, the oil flowed like water. King Saul, feeling abashed that God should choose a young boy, was equally shocked when the kingdom faced what appeared to be an impossible task: defeating Goliath, the giant. Nevertheless, this young man volunteered to fight the giant in single combat. David's triumph over his terrifying opponent was a miracle, confirmation that God chose him.

At first, Saul adopted the endearing young man and named him his heir. The king trained the boy in governance and the art of war, preparing David to succeed him when Saul died. Besides his duties to the king, David continued his devotion to prayer and worship of the Lord. Known for his beautiful voice, David sang to the Lord and spoke to him in prayer as he traveled around the kingdom. David loved the Lord first, before all others, and the Lord blessed him abundantly.

David's fame spread far and wide. The people hailed him as their hero. Jealousy, the terrible fear of being replaced, entered the heart of Saul, and he conspired to kill David. David barely escaped with his life and hid in the caves high in the mountains. The young man wept bitter tears of hurt and sorrow that the man he loved as a father would betray him. In Psalm 34, David writes touchingly of the confusion, devastation, and disappointment he felt while hiding in the cave. Honest and poignant, his prose speaks to what we all feel when betrayed by someone we love. The prophet Isaiah said it best: Don't put your trust in mere humans. They are as frail as breath. What good are they? [Isaiah 2:22 NLT]

David would survive his ordeal and fulfill the Lord's aspirations for him, defeating his enemies and uniting the kingdom of the Jews. However, he would make some egregious mistakes. These two extraordinary individuals loved God, yet they made vastly different choices concerning their fellow man. Growing up ignored and dismissed, David used the blessing of his triumph over Goliath to grow in the esteem of others and order the murder of another man to take his wife. Ultimately, the Lord forgave David but would exact a high price of atonement because of the magnitude of his sin.

Margaret was precluded from romantic relationships because of her extensive disabilities, was the object of pity by many and charity by some, but was also subject to the scorn of strangers and subjugation, torment and abuse at the hands of her father, and betrayal by her mother who failed to protect her. Nevertheless, she approached her fellow citizens graciously, generously, and with kindness. Margaret did not return eye-for-an-eye: she remained faithful to the love she shared with God and obeyed him in all things. Revered as the saint she was, Margaret of Castello, as documented, is loved by thousands of people.

Many of us choose the path of David: consciously or unconsciously, we feel justified, as victims of abuse or mistreatment, to pursue whatever pleasure we fancy. Among the adult survivors of child abuse, the National Institute on Drug Abuse (NIDA), a division of the National Institute of Health (NIH), reports 67% will become long-term drug abusers. Another study by the U.S. National Library of Medicine NIH studied 465 men and women of all races, ethnicities, and socio-economic backgrounds with a history of extensive drug abuse and treated them for detox. In querying the subjects on their family of origin, facilitators asked if the patients had suffered physical abuse or sexual abuse as children: 81% of the women and 69% of the men affirmed they had suffered from physical or sexual abuse. These patients exhibited symptoms including PTSD; significant depression, heightened in women; underlying feelings of shame and guilt; and poor impulse control, more in men than women.

Throughout his entire life, David never lost sight of the Lord; his regret over his sins was sincere. David's love of God was genuine, heartfelt, and child-like in its vulnerability, qualities we see in St. Margaret of Castello, who preferred to assist homeless children, joyfully attending to the needs of the poor, or reverently praying to the Lord on behalf of others. It was David's love of God that redeemed him. Likewise, Margaret would experience the love she missed from the low-income families who cared for her as a child and to whom she was devoted as an adult.

We see another similarity between these two: Margaret does not return her parent's mistreatment with anger or resentment; David does not utter a word of reproach towards his faithless friend, the king. Both Margaret and David correctly perceive that the immediate human response to betrayal - anger - will only perpetuate sin and divide people. The free exchange of love between God and two of his children is transformative. St. Thomas Aquinas defines love as, 'Willing the good of the other as other.' Margaret and David's love of God preserved pure love and kindness in their hearts: they do not respond to hurt, betrayal, and disappointment as we would. This more profound love, this communion with God, is impossible unless both parties know they are loved by the other. Margaret and David knew God loved them; their hearts were full, transformed, and they could love and worship Him in return. Loving God and placing Him first in your life does not change God; it changes you.

Later in the Psalm, David speaks of his love for the Lord, which has softened his heart. So then, without malice, he generously instructs us to be wise and warns future generations: 'Turn away from evil and do good. Search for peace, and work to maintain it.' [Psalm 34:14].

Born of this unabashed love for God and his certainty in his Creator's love for him, David instinctively chooses the correct path to follow:

> *I sought the Lord, who answered me*
> *and delivered me from all my fears.*
> *Those who look to him are radiant; their faces are never*
> *covered with shame.*
> *This poor man called, and the Lord heard him;*
> *he saved him out of all his troubles.*
> *The angel of the Lord encamps around those who fear him,*
> *and he delivers them.*
> Psalm 34:4-7 NIV

To answer your question, reading these verses will not erase the painful memories of a loved one's treachery, abuse, or perfidy. When we face painful duplicity or abandonment by a brother or sister, the Lord allows us to experience the gift of suffering so that we might unite with Him and the mercy of His wisdom, as recorded by His servants, especially David. If we heed the promises in this passage, these verses will aid us in responding as Jesus would and did. Jesus, the son of God, assumed a human form and, knowing us better than we know ourselves, foresaw the betrayal and unimaginable suffering He would endure. Yet, He refused to respond to the abuse in kind. Jesus prevented further harm and suffering from his sacrifice as he saved us from ourselves. And the gift to us for trusting Him not to abandon us in our pain, deliver us from our pain, and emulate His response of peace and charity to our persecutor? The achievement we hoped for: we become more like Him. We glimpse the Beatific Vision at that moment.

We give thanks for the honor of participating in God's peace plan for his children. Let us pray for the wisdom to heed the call of Jesus and to not return like, for like, an eye for an eye. May we never experience regret over memories of our angry response to betrayal and insult. Let us be merciful that we may know mercy.

Mrs. Sheppard

Chapter 3
MRS. SHEPARD

"For you have been a refuge for the poor, a refuge for the needy in their distress, a shelter from the storm and a shade from the heat. For the breath of the ruthless is like a storm driving against a wall."

[ISAIAH 25:4 NIV]

THE FATEFUL MORNING OF NOVEMBER 22, 1963, was approximately 10:30 am in Los Angeles as we sat in our classrooms. The teacher was writing something on the blackboard when the overhead speaker startled us, and we heard the principal's voice announce that "the president has been shot." My teacher screamed and crumpled into a chair. Another teacher came in crying and ran over to comfort her. Pandemonium ensued. As adults rushed about, we sat in our chairs, unsure what to do. As grammar school-age children in the early 60s, our school had drilled us endlessly on emergencies, especially the threat of Soviet missiles and nuclear attacks. But unfortunately, there was no drill for this situation. We were all too afraid to move. Finally, the nurse appeared at the door and sent us all home. Confused and scared, I walked home in silence.

I remember how sad and shocked I was to see my teacher, Mrs. Shepard, so upset. Except for my beloved Grammy, she was my favorite person. The school had been in session only a few weeks when she noticed me sitting alone outside and rarely raising my hand in class. Mrs. Shepard sat with me one day in the schoolyard, asking me why I didn't play with the other children. She noticed my bruised arm but said nothing. I saw her register my injuries, and panic ensued. The stern warnings from my father to never speak about what happened in our home were ever with me. But I also felt ashamed - *She would think I was a bad girl*. But she didn't. And from then on, we sat together every few days during recess. At first, I kept my eyes down and said little. Mrs. Shepard would sit there with me in silence and not move until it was time to go in.

Not long after we sat together at recess, she asked me to stay after school and pulled out some new books. As I leafed through them, she asked me to read some passages she had selected. I liked her books, so I read her the passages. Then, she registered some surprise and asked me to read more. I suddenly remembered my responsibilities at home, and I was late. Suddenly standing up and leaving surprised Mrs. Shepard, but she smiled and let me go.

So it began: me reading out loud or writing sentences, solving math problems, or reciting back to her the critical points of a short story. Mrs. Shepard should have corrected me when my speech faltered, or I stuttered. But instead, she waited for me to repeat myself until I could enunciate the answers correctly. My stammering continued for weeks until she asked me to take a note home to my mother. Oh no, I thought. Someone from school sending home a note was never a good thing.

Mama read the note, then re-read it. Finally, she looked over at me and back at the message. Early the next day, my parents drove me to school, a thing that hadn't happened since kindergarten. We walked to my classroom and my parents met Mrs. Shepard. After a few pleasantries, she asked me to read one of her books in the reading corner as the three of them chatted. After a few minutes, Daddy stood up and nodded; Mama just sat there momentarily, then they waved to me and left.

Everything changed. After a few days, Mrs. Shepard took me to the office, where I promptly burst into tears, promising her I wouldn't be bad anymore if she would forgive me. She hugged me close and explained that I wasn't in trouble; she had someone for me to meet. Mrs. Shepard introduced me to a kind lady and explained I would meet her for a few days to answer some questions. She advised me to take my time; she was happy to wait. I recall feeling very confused: going to the office meant notes going home and getting me in trouble. But no one seemed to look at me that ominous way this time: they did their work as the lady organized some books and papers. I answered all of her questions for several days. Then, she left for a week and returned. Mrs. Shepard returned me to the office and explained that this lady was a speech therapist. She would excuse me from lessons twice a week, and I was to come to this office to work with her.

The therapist and I worked together for weeks. Sometimes we worked on school work - reading, writing, and math problems. She made a point of placing things in my line of sight so I could read them. She once gave me a puzzle of wooden shapes and asked me to put them together. She told me she was timing the test, bringing out a little alarm clock. And, as always, she allowed me to place the work further to the right of the table, where I could see it with my one healthy eye.

In other tests, she asked me to say words, sometimes slow or sometimes fast. Or make funny sounds with my mouth. If I stuttered or faltered, she just waited until I could start again. She did not rush or make me feel foolish if I couldn't pronounce something.

Finally, she brought in some new tests and her little alarm clock. We worked on those tests - she explained, setting a timer, me working, and stopping when the little clock went off. The testing process lasted for several days. Finally, the therapist left, and Mrs. Shepard asked to speak to my parents.

My parents seemed to care about their appearance that day; Daddy wore a suit. He drove us with Mama early to school again, and as I pretended to read my book, my parents listened intently, their eyes never leaving Mrs. Shepard's face. Then, finally, Daddy and Mama stood up, nodded at me, and left. It was sunny that day but cold. I remember because Mama had worn one of her matching sweater sets. I followed Mrs. Shepard toward the front of the room, and as we sat together, she put her arm around me and told me what the tests were for.

Mrs. Shepard had suspected that I was far more intelligent than previous teachers led her to believe. Convinced my speech impediment, blindness in one eye, and other factors had contributed to my lack of expression and responsiveness. Mrs. Shepard requested permission first from the principal, then my parents, to have my I.Q. tested. The tests concluded that I was functioning at two full school years above my current third grade, with my reading and comprehension scoring even higher. The recommendation was that I advance to the combined fourth-and-fifth grade class to become familiar with the work in both grades to determine where I would fit. Meanwhile, I would continue my speech therapy throughout the school year.

My reaction was not what Mrs. Shepard expected. I said nothing. The class was about to begin. I went to my desk and, to her credit, Mrs. Shepard left me alone that day to absorb the news. As they each arrived home that night, my parents approached me tentatively as though they didn't know me. Everyone was quiet. I went to bed early. As I lay in bed, I felt small happiness: someone had taken the time to see me.

Several weeks went by as I continued working with the speech therapist and completing the additional assignments from Mrs. Shepard. Finally, one morning she asked me to step outside class and wait while she assigned something for the other students to work on. Then she and I walked a few doors down to a more extensive, two-grade classroom where the kids were working intently on something. Their teacher walked over, smiled, and welcomed me to her class. I was to sit in for an hour and see how I liked it.

Ultimately, I refused to transfer. I explained to Mrs. Shepard that the kids were much taller than me, and I felt awkward. She didn't press me and correctly surmised that, as painfully shy as I was, this change was too intimidating. The recognition of my intelligence and ability was precious, and it was because of Mrs. Shepard. I was unwilling to relinquish my class and my newfound friendship. Mrs. Shepard gave me extra reading and other work to do.

Meanwhile, my neighborhood was growing increasingly tense and scary. Daddy's visits had ceased with Mrs. Shepard's first note, but I lived with the certainty that they would begin soon. Outside, my home was unsafe; inside, my house was dangerous. School, and the time I spent with Mrs. Shepard, were my only respite.

When my parents heard of my decision, Daddy accepted it with equanimity. Mama shrugged her shoulders, "That's just like you."

The years of my parent's abuse and ridicule wore down the fabric of my being. There were moments, many times, when I just wanted to die. But, in His infinite mercy, the Lord works in mysterious ways, blessing me with the assistance of various kinds throughout my life. Mrs. Shepard was one of these. Her willingness to intervene in my education and request I.Q. and speech testing was a turning point for me: teachers and fellow students treated me differently. As a result, I saw myself in a new light.

Dysfunctional behavior patterns, established by previous generations and woven into the fabric of the family, are not easily changed. This phenomenon plays itself out in a variety of ways in families. It is not unknown to the Lord: the sin of idolatry, the worship of pagan gods and their often horrendous practices, are the subject of God's warnings in this example but are applied to our modern concerns: the sin of idolatry of parental obsessions outside the family create outward patterns of behavior and the de-prioritizing the family and their shared belief. '...I, the Lord, am your God, a jealous God, who punishes the sins of the father upon their sons to the third and fourth generation of those who hate me..' [Exodus 20:5 NCB] There can be no greater punishment than allowing us the free will to repeat the patterns of abuse, sin, and malice of our parents. The children would grow up repeating these practices with their children, further promulgating idolatry into our culture. These behavior patterns become integral to a child's formation. Children who suffer from continual abuse begin to believe they deserve it. As adults, many adult survivors of child abuse will gravitate towards a partner that will satisfy their unconscious need to be ill-treated. And so the pattern endures.

The first step for me was acknowledging the origins of my emotional pain and sharing it with a trusted friend, a therapist, and finally, a priest. For many people like me, raised to keep secrets, this may be the first time they admit to what transpired in their family.

I had to commit to a longer time to heal than I expected. Although this realization was at first discouraging, as the process continued, I began to realize that although the Lord could heal me instantly, yet doesn't, isn't because He didn't *want* to; in His wisdom, He must have known that true healing for me was a two-steps-forward-one-step-back progression. I resisted often, became frustrated, and threw up my hands. I quit several times. I was angry at Him many times. But I returned, again and again, bearing in mind the verse from Romans 8:28, 'We know that God makes all things work together for good for those who love Him and who are called according to His purpose' [Romans 8:28 NCB] To this day I remind myself of this passage, for, despite how it may appear, the Lord *is* working in my life to heal me.

Another step in my progress was recognizing that childhood pain often originated from traumatic events I did not want to remember. Many adult children of abusers experience continued upheaval in their lives and respond with heightened sensitivity and reactions: it is what is familiar. To remain peaceful, committed to the tasks of daily life, finding satisfaction in the mundane, and staying committed to daily prayer and worship is the ultimate goal in life as established by our Creator. A daily prayer and devotion habit may not appear satisfying at the outset of your journey: we want a hero to swoop in and save us. The Lord sent us a hero who did save us: Jesus. He also sent others to be disciples - us. Following in the footsteps of Jesus is the hero's path.

One of my favorite books, *Chop Wood, Carry Water,* by Rick Fields, is a perfect example of this philosophy. Full of anecdotes, stories, and the words of Jesus Christ, as well as the wisdom of ancient teachers, including the Buddha, Loa Tse, and Confucius, I read this excellent book almost 35 years ago, and it remains a highly respected guide. In another beautiful book, *The Fault of Our Stars*, John Green describes the agony of healing: "That's the thing about pain. It demands to be felt". Memories, revelations, and insights often occurred as I walked through the healing process. It was vital for me to embrace the process.

Finally, attending church and daily prayer was integral to the healing process. I learned to invite Jesus into the healing process and to surrender it to His Divine Will. Even if you assume He already knows the process you have started (which He does), inviting God into this area is an admission that you need His help and that He has the power and desire to heal you. *It was a surrender of my will to my creator.* This surrendering process took time. I thought to myself: I made it this far on my own. The challenge was to relinquish my protective shield of pride and to allow His healing power to work through me, elevating a painful past from a collection of sordid recollections to a new place, a higher plane of life, that I did not know existed.

We hear much about knowing your truth, which usually pertains to each person's version of certain events, disagreements, or feelings they experienced before, during, or after. *Feelings are not facts. Truth is a product of God, and God is Love. And like God, truth is eternal.* I know from experience that Truth and feelings are not the same. In fact, in examining a theory; reading scripture or history, and in marriage; anything I am involved in, my feelings have proven to be consistently unreliable. Feelings are like the blue sky: from our vantage point, the blue sky seems to change continually because of the weather or the time of the day. But if we travel above the Earth's atmosphere, we realize that space always appears the same. Truth is truth, no matter how we feel about it.

Walking with the Holy Spirit through the valley of suffering that can be childhood memories takes great courage. Know that the Lord is beside you; His rod and staff will comfort you. Lean on them.

The Psalmist assures us, "The Lord is near to the broken-hearted and saves the crushed in spirit." [Psalm34:18 NASB]

Like most dysfunctional families, the cycle of abuse in our home restarted. Despite unequivocal proof of my intelligence, Mama's nickname, 'Stone,' resumed. To her relief, Daddy began to see other women, occasionally returning to my bed at night.

A year later, my parents agreed that Grammy and her sister would move in with us. The Lord was sending another angel.

Chapter 4

THE QUESTION OF SUFFERING AND LOSS

Evil deeds are like a young chicken; they always come home to roost

ROBERT SOUTHEY,
prolific 19th Century English, Romantic, co-author, *The Fall of Robespierre*, Play (1794); friend of Wordsworth, admired by Byron.

By THE START OF THE fifth grade school year in September, our neighborhood was still picking up the pieces, deeply shaken from the Watts Riots a month before. Our home in East Los Angeles was on the boundary of the districts hit the worst, in what we now know as an area approximately 45 miles in circumference. Despite the unrest, I remained a latch-key kid walking to school and back with my house key pinned to the inside of my clothes. However, the first few weeks after the Riots, as soon as I arrived home from school, we stayed inside with locked doors and did not play out front with the other kids, to Daddy's orders.

My father had left construction and opened a gasoline station and a foreign car repair shop. After a severe work-related injury to his back, he closed the gasoline station and focused on his repair shop. There were many late nights, even after he hired some guys to assist him. We would bring him dinner sometimes and visit with him there.

Mama had advanced at her office as well. Her steady pay increases underwrote our living expenses and allowed Daddy to expand his business. In addition, he garnered a few reliable customers whose temperamental luxury automobiles required constant attention. One was a physician whose office was in a suburb less than 20 miles further east of our home.

Preoccupied and exhausted, whether consciously or unconsciously, Mama did not acknowledge the resumption of Daddy's nightly visits. After my momentous third-grade school year was over, Daddy had not misused me for over a year. Even in family conversations, he seemed reticent to speak to me. But my parents arguing had returned, especially after the Riots. As their fighting escalated, Daddy stayed at work later and later, arriving long after we all were in bed. Tired and lonely, he periodically returned to my bunk bed at night and resumed his visits.

One of Daddy's visits did not turn out quite the same as others. Daddy's resumption of his nightly visits to my bunk bed always began the same way: middle of the night, slowly turning the doorknob, checking my sister, then wordlessly climbing into my bunk and rolling me towards the wall. As Daddy fumbled with the covers, I closed my eyes and cried, silently praying to Jesus to take me now. Let me die. As Daddy proceeded, and it hurt, a light in my mind's eye, not bright but soft, shone, and I could feel that I was not alone. Someone was there with me. *Take me!* I silently pleaded. The light did not waver as it grew closer. Then it was all I saw. No sound. No tremble. Just peace. I was physically still in the bunk bed next to Daddy, but the light had taken me somewhere else in my mind. And then it was over. I noticed my surroundings again and could hear Daddy standing up, sighing. Then he left. And I was ok. I was peaceful. At that moment, I felt a calm certainty: I know I will be ok no matter what happens.

Not long after that night, I started experiencing symptoms of vaginitis. Mama, angry and frustrated with me, unsuccessfully treated it with over-the-counter creams. Finally, forced to take me to the doctor, Daddy sent us to his customer, the physician whose office was in the suburbs. I remember they ushered us into an exam room with metal stirrups on either side of the examination table. As I scrambled up, the nurse helped place my feet properly, had me remove my panties, and draped a sheet over my legs and abdomen. I was ten years old. Mama was silent as a tall, skinny man with all-white hair and a white lab coat walked in. I turned my head away as the doctor sat on a low stool, folded the sheet back, and peered between my legs. As tears welled in my eyes, I turned away and cried quietly.

Unbeknownst to my mother, this doctor was also a bishop of his protestant faith. Within seconds of examining my condition, he let out a growl, stood up, and confronted my mother, asking her who had done this to me and stating that he intended to report my condition to the police. Cowering in a corner, Mama burst into tears and begged the doctor not to report my situation to anyone. She sobbed so hard and loud the doctor became alarmed, and after a few minutes, he relented, cleansed me, and wrote my mother two prescriptions: one for me, one for Daddy. Then, he gathered his things and left the room without looking at me. I left that office red-faced and ashamed. I wasn't exactly sure what had just happened or what I had done, but instinctively, I knew that whatever was wrong was my fault.

I recall the tension between my parents that night. After they put us to bed, I snuck down the hall and peered into the living room. Mama sat next to Daddy on the couch and, in hushed tones, related the day's events. The only part of the conversation I could hear was Mama admitting to the terror at the idea that I could eventually become pregnant or have Daddy arrested. How my mother started this conversation, how Daddy found it within himself to acknowledge their dilemma, and for them to continue living together as husband and wife, and for all of us to go on as a family is beyond me.

After that day, Daddy's visits stopped. My father, already a mercurial personality, was irritable and angry, becoming agitated over the slightest irritation. He was deprived of the emotional outlet he depended upon, and the pressure built. Mama retreated further from their relationship, isolating herself in her bedroom. Embarrassed by the doctor's reaction, humiliated by his wife's cold daily silence, and with no other outlet for his pent-up feelings, Daddy externalized his anger. He relieved his frustration by beating me with his belt over the slightest infraction. Soon after I healed from the mysterious infection, my menstruation inexplicably began. At ten years old, Mama commented that it was a little early for it to start and showed me all the feminine equipment and how to use it. This new development gave rise to another hushed conversation between my parents. And the beatings continued.

Looking back upon it, the incidences of my father's violence seemed to have no particular pattern: I could never predict what might set him off. I tried applying my child's reasoning to his behavior to determine the best way to avoid a whipping: *Should I be more helpful around the house? Better yet, do not ask for anything. Stay silent and fade into the woodwork.* Weeks of apparent harmony would suddenly transform into the apocalypse of Daddy's anger, igniting and exploding without warning. During these episodes, Mama would run and hide in their bedroom, locking the door, leaving my sister and me, caught in my father's madness, to fend for ourselves. Daddy terrified Mama, yet he never hit her, and she never protected me.

And madness it was. Madness is the only feasible explanation for my father's behavior—complete insanity. As time elapsed, the school nurse, teachers, and, one time, a principal all sent home notes about bloody legs and purple bruises. Mama threw away the letters, anticipating that the school officials would behave as other adults around us did: not wanting to know the full extent of what they suspected, each of them soon forgetting about the episode or failing to follow up and never reporting. They proved Mama right.

I continued to use silence to deal with what was happening in our family. Whatever occurred in my home, I never spoke about it. Speech seemed almost impossible to me. If I uttered even one word, I risked disclosure. Finally, my parents made it plain to me that admitting the truth to someone outside the family was tantamount to betrayal, earning a slap from my mother for shaming our family or, at worst, a beating with the belt from my father.

The other lesson on interpersonal relations I garnered from these experiences is that, as I prolonged my silent isolation, my peers, noticing the bruises and fat lips, tacitly avoided me. They didn't want to know, and I don't blame them.

Within weeks of the physician's exam, Mama told us that Grandma Eva - my beloved Gram - and her sister, my Great Aunt Clarice, were moving from Sacramento and would join us. Given Mama's history with Gram, that Gram had left my grandfather immediately after discovering he had molested Mama when she was eight years old, I am convinced that Mama must have turned to her in her distress. Decisive and fearless,

Grammy immediately chose to sell her home and move south. Mama seemed relieved; Daddy said nothing and sulked.

God bless Grammy forever.

In contemplating the appalling panorama of human sin, we are all united in our hatred of the mistreatment of children. When a member of the audience asks me how I survived these experiences, I ask the audience, how did you survive a terrible divorce? The death of your child? Loss of your job? Betrayal in marriage? We mustn't compare our trials with another's: we can recite moments we have suffered, and, most likely, we will suffer again in this life. Our Blessed Redeemer stated the facts emphatically and promised not to abandon us: 'These things I have spoken to you, so that in Me you may have peace. In the world, you have tribulation, but take courage; I have overcome the world.' [John 16:33 NASB]

The question of human suffering and loss, our great existential dilemma, has confused and disheartened humanity for as long as we have existed on Earth. From philosophers to farmers, titans to teachers; whether rich or poor; from every walk of life, we have searched for an answer to the question, *Why do these tragedies happen to us? Why must we suffer so dreadfully in this life?*

Every day I witness the faith of heroes who have overcome terrible loss, enduring unimaginable suffering, yet are faithful to the Lord. Any random thought of heroes immediately brings to mind friends of mine from church, Carlos and Catherine del Castillo, the Gold Star parents of a son killed in combat in Afghanistan. This brave couple embodies a faithful walk with God, which I hope to emulate.

Catherine and Carlos' son, Dmitri del Castillo, graduated from West Point, receiving his second lieutenant commission as a 2nd lieutenant. After additional training, he earned the US Army Ranger tab and Airborne wings, completing Ranger School. Lieutenant del Castillo served in Afghanistan, dying under heavy enemy fire as he attempted to radio for additional backup to save his brothers. Under heavy fire, he refused to relinquish that mike. In recognition of his outstanding service to his country, the military decorated Dmitri multiple times, including, but not limited to, the Bronze Star, the Purple Heart, and the Army Commendation Medal. This courageous soldier loved his family, helped others in need, and died in the service of his country. No parent could ever be prouder of a child than Catherine and Carlos are of Dmitri.

The living testimony of the power of God in the lives of the del Castillo's is apparent to me because of their proximity: each time I see them at church, my heart lifts, and I am thankful that they call me a friend. In my formation as a Christian, the Lord has challenged me to seek other brave families like the del Castillo's who, although the suffering is unique in each situation, all the families are alike in one specific way: they chose life. Mustering all the courage required in any battle, these families bravely place one foot in front of the other after the tragedy.

Taking part with others in volunteer and charitable endeavors who have loved and lost or suffered some other devastation has become one of the greatest gifts I've received from God: service to others was my ladder out of a deep hole of sadness and despair. We all can bear witness to the mighty works of the Lord in healing: it eased the pain of my suffering by participating in helping to relieve the suffering of others. And all I had to do was agree to help.

Father Jean C. D'Elbee speaks of this accurate determination in his book, I Believe in Love, noting that even committed or advanced Christians *'have fallen because they failed to endure an injustice and exaggerated it.'* I have no doubts that the Del Castillo family endured long days of almost unimaginable pain and that their grief is still very present. To honor their son and give life to Dmitri's highest aspirations, the del Castillos established a scholarship fund in their son's name. Their loss has become the springboard for various charitable endeavors close to their child's heart. The spirit of that brave lieutenant, Dmitri del Castillo, lives on. I, too, may one day be measured against their faith and love and not be found wanting.

The most painful experience, more painful than my father's abuse, was the realization that came to me much later, after years of prayer, journaling, and therapy: the recognition that it was my mother's abandonment and betrayal that lay at the root of my deepest pain and ultimately the source of my lack of faith. My-father-the-monster-beleaguering-me and my poor mother was the mental scenario I played out well into my thirties. But, unfortunately, it took much uncovering to face the facts: my father could not have repeated his crimes over the years without my mother's complicit acceptance. The guilt she felt over the multiple incidents of molestation, beating, and verbal abuse inflicted upon me as a child must have overwhelmed her: she sought treatment for depression from her physician, who prescribed medication she later became addicted to, and, in her desperation to end her psychic pain, attempted to end her life multiple times. Ultimately, Mama doubled my pain by forcing me to be her lifesaver and caretaker. The years I remained in denial, refusing to face her betrayal, speak to how painful this recognition was. And I used the pain of Mama's betrayal as an excuse to avoid trusting Jesus: if she didn't love me, how could he?

How do we answer the question of human suffering? How did I survive–and thrive–after overwhelming circumstances? In the comforting peace of obedience to the commandments of God, I was finally and truly free. Free of anxiety, guilt, shame, fear, and regret. Jesus admonishes us to forgive if we want to be forgiven; in the face of insult and injury, not to respond in kind but to turn the other cheek. I have applied this commandment from God into a simple maxim I dedicate my life to: *to recover from childhood trauma or any suffering or loss, we must give the love we did not receive.* This maxim applies in contemplating the forgiveness of a perpetrator as well. Eventually, I found no way to move forward in life without this crucial step. Forgiveness does not equate to absolution: each abusive, neglectful parent or person must own up to their mistakes. And if they don't, I leave their judgment to Jesus.

This step was even more difficult than it sounds. I could not have done it; I would not have attempted it without the grace of God. Simply not possible. With the mercy and grace of Jesus, it took a series of steps over several years to pardon first my father, then my mother. Learning the truth about how they grew up and the pain they carried was a needful first step.

Living the life of a faithful Christian is hard. Christ calls us to a life of sacrifice: his apostles freely admitted, as his followers, what we can expect, "After you have suffered for a little while, the God of all grace, who called you to His eternal glory in Christ, will himself perfect, confirm, strengthen and establish you." [1 Peter 2:20 ESV]

Writer Brian Pizzalato speaks of this in his article, *Christ Gives Meaning to Suffering,* 'In our own suffering, Christ allows us to share in the deepest sign of his love. He has infused suffering with divine meaning, not human meaninglessness. Human suffering is thus redeemed. Through our suffering, we participate in the sacrifice of Christ, which brings about our salvation and the salvation of others.

As a new Christian first baptized, the word *sacrifice* was an anathema to me: hadn't I suffered enough? Over the years, I began to recognize that suffering is an integral part of the composite that defines the human condition because *suffering is indelibly linked to love. One cannot exist without the other.* As Catholics, we recognize that life contains desolations and consolations. It was my Catholicism that helped me to understand that suffering had a purpose: it is redemptive. In suffering, we not only emulate Christ, but we can also become Christ-like. Archbishop Luis M. Martinez articulates clearly for us this very tenet of the Holy Spirit, "[The Holy Spirit's] ideal is to reproduce Jesus in us, and through Jesus and with Jesus, to take us to the bosom of the Trinity and glorify the Father with the supreme glorification of Jesus.…. Through the shadows of faith, we…. try to get a glimpse of this divine work, to see how, under the influence of the Holy Spirit, souls are purified, illuminated, and enkindled until they are transformed into Jesus, the soul, the glorious summit of the mystical ascent where we find peace and happiness – where we find God."

I've also come to acknowledge that true and lasting change cannot occur without the silence of contemplation and communion with God. Restless souls, lurching from one influence after another, cannot integrate the truth inherent in the Gospels if they do not spend significant time in prayerful contemplation. Surrendering to the spirit in meditation and prayer signals an inner shift has occurred: a true trusting of the Holy Spirit has overtaken the anxious Christian; the Doubting Thomas freely submits to a knowing higher power. Without this investment of time in quiet examination, the fleeting glimpses of truth, grasped as we journey to the next experience, may not take root within the soul. Jesus imparts this pivotal point in His teaching of the parable of the sower (Matthew 13:1-23 NCB): seeds planted indiscriminately by a distracted sower are easily disrupted by the wind of fretful endeavor and obsessive worrying, keeping the soul forever locked in the treadmill of often helpful, but distracting, industry, ever chained to an underlying dysthymic sadness at the fruitlessness of life.

My beloved Grammy related a sort of proverb to me years ago, and I never forgot it: *the things of God are often hard in the beginning and easy in the end; the things that are not of God are easy in the beginning and hard in the end.* Why? Does He want this to be difficult? God does not contemplate that. As C. S. Lewis states in his book **Mere Christianity**, 'He wants us to love and be loved.' The sooner we choose to love and be loved, the less we suffer. In his brilliant book, *I Believe in Love, Father D'Elbee*, speaks of the Lord's having deliberately "*allow[ed] us to endure the struggles which humiliate us, for they are precious. Often, he will leave you the trial, he will leave you the humiliation, but he will help you stay united to his will in the very center of the storm*".

Again, it came down to my choices: there it was, that pesky free will again. Consciously or unconsciously, I was choosing to be slightly miserable most of the time. *I discovered that change was only as complicated as deciding.* Was it Jesus' plan for me to suffer the pain of watching my mother try to kill herself? To feel resentful for her abandonment of me for over 40 years? No. His plan was for me to pardon each person who wronged me, to see the Christ within them, forgiving their trespasses as he forgives mine. His goal was for me to love my mother and forgive her, despite the pain she caused me, and to believe she loved me as much as possible. It was Jesus' plan that I know and believe that He always has, and always will, love me completely. Not an outcome I would ever have dreamed of on my own.

My formation as a Catholic has led me to a quiet place of internal examination, gratitude, and knowingness. By praying the Rosary, I have begun a relationship with our Blessed Mother: her generosity in meeting each believer where they are is at once precious, as it is miraculous. *She just knows.* Our Lady guided me ever so gently to the foot of the Cross, where I laid my broken spirit, my burdensome resentment, and my overwhelming sadness at Jesus' broken, bleeding feet. Each time I pray the Rosary, I return to the Cross with our Blessed Mother; her reassuring presence taking each step with me.

Our Lord invites us to share His suffering, for in His Passion and Crucifixion, Jesus elevates the suffering itself. St. John Paul II addressed this essential question of the meaning and purpose of suffering most eloquently in his magnificent apostolic letter, *Salvici Doloris*, "As a result of Christ's salvific work, man exists on earth *with the hope* of eternal life and holiness. And even though the victory over sin and death achieved by Christ in his Cross and Resurrection does not abolish temporal suffering from human life, nor free from suffering the whole historical dimension of human existence, it nevertheless *throws a new light* upon this dimension and upon every suffering: the light of salvation. This is the light of the Gospel, that is, of the Good News. The truth expounded in the conversation with Nicodemus is at the heart of this light: "For God so loved the world that he gave his only Son"(31). This truth radically changes the picture of man's history and his earthly situation: in spite of the sin that took root in this history both as an original inheritance and as the "sin of the world" and as the sum of personal sins, God the Father has loved the only-begotten Son, that is, he loves him in a lasting way; and then in time, precisely through this all-surpassing love, he "gives" this Son, that he may strike at the very roots of human evil and thus draw close in a salvific way to the whole world of suffering in which man shares."

The powerful words, '…He may strike at the very roots of human evil…' caught my breath: our suffering is *redemptive* – the means by which Jesus liberates us from the ultimate agony: eternal damnation. In our pain, we are invited to *participate* with Jesus in saving the world. St. John Paul II further explains, "First of all, He *blots out* from human history *the dominion of sin,* which took root under the influence of the evil Spirit, beginning with Original Sin, and then He gives man the possibility of living in Sanctifying Grace. In the wake of His victory over sin, He also takes away the dominion *of death,* by his resurrection beginning the process of the future resurrection of the body. Both are essential conditions of "eternal life", that is of man's definitive happiness in union with God; this means, for the saved, that in the eschatological perspective suffering is totally blotted out."

This essential Christian truth finally gelled in my mind when I started to study Latin and discovered the origin of the verb to suffer: *sufferer* - to undergo a passage. Passage: the temporary path leading to an opening, not *permanent.* My temporal travails are just that: temporary. And they had meaning; there was *a purpose* and *sufficiency to my suffering.* Jesus became the example of what is best in men and solved the most incredible mercy: Jesus lived a blameless life amongst us, and we killed Him for it. Yet to

His very last breath, the Son of God chose to love and forgive those who had sinned beyond human forgiveness. Jesus is the template for achieving our purpose on Earth.

As always, the Lord does not force our hand; he knows we are spiritual toddlers trapped in our earthly bodies, removed from His presence, and will not readily choose to suffer. The two-year-old learning to speak loves to say no. They are the ultimate contrarians. In our limited understanding, we want to follow our inclination: unless *we feel it*, chances are *we won't do it*. No human being ever *feels like* suffering. The life and death of Lieutenant Dimitri Del Castillo is a clear example of a conscience choice to sacrifice, born of the purest love the Lord places in each of our hearts, compelling him to turn towards suffering and stand his ground in the face of overwhelming odds.

Gold Star parents, Carlos and Catherine Del Castillo, were powerless to prevent the loss of their beloved son. Yet, every day, in the face of enduring grief and devastating loss, this brave family marches forward to help others. They refuse to drop the mike.

Three generations enveloped in this tragedy, my beloved Grammy, her sister, Aunt Clarice, Mama, and me

Chapter 5

GRAM

Gray hair is a crown of glory; it is gained by a righteous life.

PROVERBS 16:31 NCB

I MET MY MATERNAL GRANDFATHER WHEN I was four or five years old, just a year before he died. Lonely, alcoholic, and destitute, living in a sad tiny residential home provided by the state, his few belongings stacked neatly and entirely contained in one room. It is doubtful that Mama ever dared to confront her father for molesting her as a child, but I know he lived and died lonely and discouraged. A Roman Catholic, he left his one treasured possession, an ivory rosary, to my mother upon his death. After my conversion, she passed it on to me. Having experienced the wondrous mystery in the ways of the Lord, it did not seem a coincidence to me that I, a victim of child molestation, should inherit a symbol of Christ and the Virgin Mary from a perpetrator. Receiving that rosary at the time that I did, when I was first embarking upon my walk with Christ, reassured me that I had heard from my Savior that *you are on the right path and continue your way. The sins of the family are over.* Holding it in my hand, I knew in my heart that the Lord had *sent* this rosary to me, confirming my grandfather's redemption. I carried it to the beach and, as the waves washed over my feet, imagined my grandfather seated at the foot of Christ, having admitted his sin to his Maker, is now forgiven and blessed. Christ lived within my grandfather, and I hold on to that. Through the auspices of a priest, I would later gift it to another man in similar circumstances, praying that he was comforted by it and redeemed by Our Savior.

During World War II, to support my mother and help the family recover from the Great Depression, Gram left Denver with her grown niece Jessie to seek work in California as a 'Rosie the Riveter,' faithfully sending money home each payday. Later on, after the war, her superior cooking skills landed her a coveted position as an original Betty Crocker, developing and testing new recipes. Grammy married twice again, outliving her two successive husbands, who lived and died loving this wonderful, faithful, intelligent, kind woman.

I remember one summer traveling to Grammy's home in Sacramento by train with Mama; she stayed one night and then left me with Grammy for a two-week visit. During that visit, I met Aunt Clarice, Gram's younger sister. A flapper in the 1920s and 1930s, the lovely Clarice had morphed into a grumpy alcoholic, sipping whisky the entire day and playing solitaire for hours.

Gram would return home from running a high school cafeteria, cook something delicious, and then spend the evening sewing Barbie clothes for our dolls with matching dresses for us. I still remember the red and white fabric with umbrellas that I picked out. We were so proud of those dresses! Later in my life, after Mama remarried and moved out of state, my grandmother's love and friendship still living nearby sustained me.

During my third-grade school year, my grandmother sold her big house in Sacramento, and she and her sister moved into our two-bedroom, one-bath duplex in Los Angeles. These two old ladies endured the discomfort of our pullout couch for almost a year before my parents scraped together enough money to move to a three-bedroom duplex in the suburbs. I now believe that somehow, from 500 miles away, and despite my mother's reluctance to speak truthfully about my father's behavior, my grandmother guessed the full extent of my father's shenanigans and moved in to intercede.

My speech problem became a significant impediment before she and Aunt Clarice arrived. Grammy tried to talk to me, encouraging me to speak to her, to open up a bit. My teacher, Mrs. Shepard, suggested speech therapy, and Grammy encouraged my parents to allow me to start treatment sessions. I enjoyed the time with my speech therapist and the one–to–one time my teacher carved out of her busy day for me. Gram living with us was also very comforting. For the entire time Grammy and her sister slept on our pullout couch, Daddy's visits at night stopped.

A subsequent family move to Whittier, a suburb of Los Angeles, coincided with an expansion of my father's business: he now owned an auto repair shop, a gas station, and a more extensive auto repair center near our new home. Daddy later expanded the more oversized garage to include auto parts, sales of refurbished classic cars, and occasional buy-here-pay-here auto financing. By this time, Aunt Clarice's alcoholism became unmanageable; her condition forced Grammy to move her to a secure living center. An enduring mystery in the family lore is why Grammy worked for Daddy in the auto parts department, helping the customers for a minimal salary; Grammy was financially independent. Daddy, a flagrant philanderer, who spent a portion of his days openly pursuing women with expensive lunches and gifts, must have made my grandmother a little nervous about our security; perhaps Grammy was monitoring the money. I returned to being home alone in the afternoons, left to my own devices.

After relocating to suburbia, Grammy purchased a small mobile home nearby. As soon as she moved out of the third bedroom and I moved in, Daddy's nightly visits resumed, although his primary focus remained with other women.

Daddy arrived unexpectedly early one afternoon and flew into another rage over I-don't-know-what and grabbed my arm, throwing me face down on the couch. Mama ran screaming to her bedroom and locked the door. As he held me down with his knee, Daddy removed his belt and battered me with the buckle end on the back and legs.

Grammy had left work and was on her way to visit with friends. She recalled later that, driving down the street, she heard a voice instructing her to go to our house immediately. Making an immediate U-turn, Grammy arrived at our home within minutes. As she entered the front door, she witnessed my father beating me, blood running down my legs, arms, and back. Grammy wedged herself in front of my father and, stretching her arms out, screamed, "Don't hurt this child!" My father snarled he would beat her if she didn't step away. In an instant, Grammy pivoted and threw her body over mine, holding me tight as the belt struck my grandmother on the shoulders. She placed her arms and legs over mine as more blows came down, shielding my body. Grammy was taking my beating. One lashing across her upper arms left a cut deep enough to bleed. Finally, after just a few more lashes, my father seemed to come to his senses and stopped.

As soon as he calmed down, Daddy left the house for the rest of the evening. Grammy and I sat on the bathtub's edge as I bandaged her wounds. Then, as she rechecked me for bleeding, I cried quietly on her shoulder. I told her how sorry I was, that it was all my fault Daddy had hurt her. Grammy squeezed me tight and told me to hush. After that, we never spoke of it again.

God granted me the grace of the love of my grandmother. He extended himself through her to me; I have carried that blessing my entire life. Even now, when I imagine what St. Michael and the heavenly angels must look like, I see my beloved Gram shining down upon me, her blessed face, the embodiment of protective love—pure and true.

Each of us carries the kindness we received from someone in the worst moments of our lives. Their service brightens the dark corners of experiences we worried we might not get through. Prayer and reflection have helped me to recognize that this kindness is of Christ. God is happy to use our brother or sister to extend a physical presence of His love to us when we need it. This same light, shining as a beacon, is the light of His kingdom living within us—a spiritual lighthouse illuminating our way as we cross the treacherous waters of earthly life.

My grandmother was brave, selfless, and about the most Christian woman the Lord ever put on this Earth. Energetic and determined, Grammy embodied the strength of the Great War generation. Perhaps she needed more patience with loafers or the unwillingness of some people to face facts and get on with it. She never really understood my mother, her daughter, at all. Nevertheless, Grammy tried very hard to live her Christian faith, and she died with her firm belief in the grace of God. The love of my Grammy lives on within me and is as present to me today as the day she saved me from that beating.

The psalmist comforts us with the knowledge of God's ever-present protection, reminding us in Psalm 91, *'...for he will order his angels to care for you and guard you wherever you go.'* [Psalm 91:11 CJB]

Shortly after the beating incident, Grammy, who had been a widow for 20 years after the death of Grandpa Joe, her second husband, met a lovely gentleman and remarried. Visiting California from his home in Helena, Montana, Grandpa Les and Grammy sold their small home and purchased another nearby. They split their time between the two residences, Montana and California, until Grandpa died. After she remarried, Grammy pointedly stayed away from our home; to see them, we visited their house. Grammy had made her point. She knew the beatings continued but were intermittent, less savage, and often months apart. Grammy's protection covered me like one of her crocheted shawls. She had marked me with her blood; I was hers.

Later, when I read the Passion narrative in the Gospel of Luke, I thought about my grandmother. My harrowing experience cowering under my grandmother's body for protection as Grammy took the blows intended for me demonstrated the depth and breadth of love in ways that perhaps very few people may have experienced. I also learned that, despite my mother's indifference, there are people in your life you can count on who will go to great lengths and suffer tremendous sacrifices for you, even if you don't think you deserve it.

As I read the Bible, I learned Grammy was not the only one to take a beating and bleed for me. Someone else loved me as much as she did and sacrificed even more for me. He lost his life to save me. And His blood shields me now.... *the Lord is faithful, and He will strengthen and protect you.* [2 Thessalonians 3:3 NASB]

Although this statement may sound fantastical, I now understand that the incidents of Daddy's beatings that the Lord allowed me to suffer had a higher purpose: had I not witnessed my courageous grandmother risk serious injury as well as possibly losing her relationship with my mother and her granddaughters, as well as the enduring enmity of my father, to save me, I could not testify that this kind of love *does* exist. But I did. And this kind of love is real. So, when friends and acquaintances want to share the testimony of Jesus' sacrifice with you, be willing to hear that story with a fresh perspective. You can count on the love of Jesus and his surrender to His enemies, absorbing blow after blow, to save you. *Jesus loves you as no one else can. Believe it. Rest in it. It is true.*

For God so loved the world, that He gave his only Son, that whoever believes in Him should not perish but have eternal life. [John 3:16 NASB]

Recently, I added a step to my nightly prayers: I count all the ways Jesus blessed me that day. Knowing I am unworthy by my actions, yet filled with gratitude for His love and mercy, I pray a 400-year-old prayer:

'Grant me, O Lord, through your bitter Passion and death, the grace to know and love your infinite goodness, to thank you and have compassion for you, for your sufferings on my behalf. Awaken in me a lively sorrow for my sins, and help me for the future to do your holy will.'

St. Paul of the Cross, 18th-century priest.

*My mother, aged 8 years old, after her parents had split
and the incident with her father, Grandpa Ray*

Chapter 6

MAMA

But none of these alms is greater than the forgiveness from the heart of a sin committed against us by someone else.

ST. AUGUSTINE OF HIPPO,
Enchiridion

*M*AMA WAS AN ENIGMA. IF the National Geographic Society and the Guinness Book of World Records had any inkling of my mother's existence, Mama would've been in the top 10 world mysteries between the Lost City of Atlantis and the Bermuda Triangle. Instead, evidencing a combination of self-possession with a distinct stillness, at once lovely but unapproachable, Mama may not have been the first person you would notice in a crowded room but notice her you would. With translucent skin and opal blue eyes, her face possessed a pronounced delicacy. Mama was lovely in a Qing-dynasty-porcelain way: beautiful to look at, almost iridescent, but it made one nervous about holding it for more than just a moment; it is best to leave it placed where it is and admire it from afar. Mama preferred her human interaction, even the admirers, kept at a distance.

Her natural detachment communicated itself very clearly to her immediate family. Wounded and alone, I craved her affection and acceptance, neither of which did she bestow with any regularity. As she was often physically ill, her detachment appeared to be a symptom of her fragility: I would approach her with some trepidation, constantly afraid to upset or 'tire' her.

Mama seemed to like me more as I grew older and could function independently. My mother worked downtown all week, so most of our housework we completed on Saturday mornings. I was allowed to watch cartoons until 9:00 am. Mama would switch off the T.V. and turn on a local F.M. radio station that played only classical music, offering a selection of operas each Saturday morning. As I dusted furniture and scrubbed the bathrooms, Maria Callas performing *Habanera* would waft through the house. Mama had her favorites, with Mario Lanza at the top. (I remember being surprised to see his picture on the front of an album for 'The Student Prince' – he looked much like my father and Uncle Dan.) As the program did not air the entire libretto, we would finish the house and the opera by lunchtime and change our clothes. Mama would take me for an egg salad sandwich at the luncheon counter in the basement of Hinshaw's, a department store in town. Mama would let me wear sheer lip gloss and carry a purse, and I remember feeling so immensely grown up.

Daddy worked on Saturday, so the housework-with-opera-then-egg-salad-and-purses ritual became our routine. Eventually, however, Daddy would arrive, and Mama would physically leave the room, her complete disdain for my father evident to both of us. Mama would retreat within herself – almost imploding–when he returned home. She couldn't bear to be around him. He would wander to the family room and flip on the T.V.; I would escape to my bedroom, thankful for the respite.

Despite the years of recovery and healing, the grace of Jesus Christ, and the intervention of the Holy Spirit, as I grew older, I occasionally heard my mother's voice saying, *C'mon, Stone, hurry up!* I spent years of my adult life alternatively angry with my mother or worried about her mental health and well-being. When she called and needed something, I was there consistently. Fred and I enjoyed a period of abundance. We sent Mama and my stepfather, Bud, on expensive European trips and cruises to distant locales, upgraded their home with all-new appliances, and treated them with beautiful gifts. However, every time we did something nice for them, Mama would complain—there was always something wrong: the hotel room was cramped, the coats we purchased for them were the wrong color, or the plane ride was uncomfortable. Mama, unhappy most of her life, her misery exacerbated by her marital discord with my stepfather, descended into another period of severe clinical depression. Later, Mama admitted she and my stepfather had both sought relationships outside of their marriage; when my mother's companion died suddenly, she was distraught. In reflecting upon Mama and the course of her life, I am reminded of a passage in the novel, *The Memoirs of a Geisha*, wherein the main character, Chiyo Sakamoto, plaintively observes, "The heart dies a slow death, shedding each hope like leaves until one day there are none. No hopes. Nothing remains."

I remember receiving a call about 20 years ago from my stepfather that he had found Mama almost dead from another suicide attempt. This time, she had swallowed an entire bottle of her heart medication and had slipped into a coma. When I arrived at her home in Oklahoma the next day, she was recovering in the hospital and was due to be sent home in a few days.

Her return home was a subdued affair. She didn't want to speak to us and refused to answer any questions. Finally, since she was eating very little and sleeping around the clock, I agreed with my stepfather to return home and allow him to care for her. While packing up my suitcase, she called me to her bedside. Mama said she wanted to confide in me the facts surrounding this episode. I listened intently, expecting to hear some recognition of the error in her thinking or an embarrassed apology for all the fuss and worry. But instead, she made it clear that 'her life was over, and it had all been pointless.' Then Mama proceeded to retell the harrowing story of the day I was born, a story Mama imparted many times when I was growing up, wielding her sad tale like a weapon, when I annoyed her or if she felt guilty about something.

When they were first married, Daddy and Mama lived in a hilly Los Angeles section facing some of the oldest parts of town, near the University of Southern California. Boyle Heights, as it was known, was initially settled by Jewish immigrants after WWII, who had vacated the area for the loftier environs of the West Side. Newly arrived immigrants from South America, Asia, and Mexico, as well as Americans from out of state, each family traveling from far and wide, seeking the highly touted opportunity available in the Golden State. Before the County of Los Angeles built the enormous present-day complex of the County/

USC Medical Center, smaller state and county-funded hospitals were available, dotting the surrounding blocks. As with all facilities like this one, Lincoln Memorial, where I was born, was plagued by short staffing, a busy emergency room crowded with very sick people, and labor and delivery departments teeming with women in the throes of childbirth, ready to deliver. I was an entire month early; Mama was rushed home from work and admitted on an emergency basis. Thankfully she could secure a bed in a large ward that, by happenstance, had discharged almost all of its recent new mothers. I am sure the overworked nurses did their best to provide her with the care she needed; however, it was a hectic afternoon, and Mama was mainly left alone.

Sometime during the early evening, Mama experienced excruciating pain and could feel blood spurting from the birth canal. She called out as best she could, but no one aided her. Mama could feel herself drift into unconsciousness. She said she 'went to the sea shore,' an area she was deathly afraid of, and waded into the water. Mama recalled that the sun was shining, its light dappling the water. No one else was there; she was alone, yet despite her fear of drowning, she felt safe and peaceful. Mama continued to wade into the water; as it reached her waist, she heard a voice instructing her to wade towards a wooden pier further down the beach. She told me she knew it would all be over when she reached the dock. Mama described a certainty to that moment; she felt ready. There was no fear, only peace. As she drew nearer, the pier now just a few yards away, the water began to swirl around her legs. Then, she looked up at the sun and suddenly woke up on a surgical gurney, with doctors and nurses hovering over her, shouting, obviously worried. I was born via Caesarian section. After two hours in recovery, and because of the influx of emergent patients, Mama was allowed to continue to recover in her room. Unfortunately, the hospital staff had not cleaned the area yet, so Mama could see the blood-soaked bed, her blood pooling underneath it. They brought her a clean bed, and she slept through the night, seeing me for the first time the next day.

When the nurses finally brought me to her, her face fell: my left eye was damaged and crossed. The doctor assured her I was a healthy baby. However, I would never see out of that eye. Each retelling of this story ended with her recounting her disappointment; after everything she had been through, she was 'saddled' with a child suffering from a congenital disability.

As with each retelling of this story, my heart sank. Mama's pregnancy had ruined her chances of leaving a marriage she deeply regretted, and my birth had almost killed her. She was sure she was being punished by having a child with a congenital problem. She felt trapped and never forgave me. Looking up from her pillow, Mama asked me why I had bothered to come.

I told her I loved her and wanted her to be happy. And that her suicide attempt had scared us all. At that moment, I felt sad for both of us estranged and told her so. Mama then told me that the one bright moment in her life recently was when my father died a few years ago. She chuckled and murmured that she had 'fixed his wagon' by refusing to tell his family where my sister and I lived so that he could see us one last time. Shocked and angry at the news I was hearing for the first time, I asked her why she refused to let them know how to contact us; she said to me, "C'mon Stone, you know why. He didn't *deserve* to see you."

I flew back to Los Angeles, furious, sad, and stunned. For months, I had been working on healing from my childhood, and my mother, aware of all the complex, painful, yet transformative work I had put in and still had not allowed me my one last chance to confront my father before he died.

After this incident, my relationship with Mama continued as before. Fred and I continued to assist them often, and we would occasionally visit them or fly them to Los Angeles to see us. A couple of years after the overdose incident, Bud mentioned that they had created a Trust during a visit to Oklahoma City. Should something happen to them, they nominated me as their trustee. Soon after this visit, Mama suffered a severe heart attack and underwent quintuple heart bypass surgery. During my visit to her bedside, they brought up the Trust again. However, as time passed and Mama seemed to recover her health again, I forgot about the Trust, and Bud didn't bring it up again. I hadn't realized they were becoming more cantankerous, obstinate, and eccentric. A painful realization of their situation came when Fred and I tried to purchase a new car for them. They became angry with us over signing the bill of sale to take possession of the vehicle, mystifyingly refusing to speak to us for almost a year.

A surprising call came from a family member informing me that social services had removed them from their home and placed them in a nursing facility for their safety. After contacting and speaking to my sister, the social worker gained access to the house and came across the trust paperwork and my nomination. After hearing a complete account of the events, I knew I needed to travel to their home immediately to check on my parents, meet with social services, and determine the next steps.

What I found appalled me. I couldn't open the front door of my parent's house as the accumulated trash had barred the entrance. Filth, bugs, mice, and human and dog excrement were everywhere. After receiving the forms I needed for an emergency court appearance from the social worker and the house keys, my faithful husband and I cleaned the home. Two hundred eighty-six 50-gallon garbage bags, bagged for three days, spoke to my parents' dire straits.

And so it began. Our home in Tennessee had just sold, and it became apparent that we had to transfer to Oklahoma City to live there for an extended time. So we placed our remaining household goods in a storage pod, and with two dogs in tow, we decamped to Oklahoma.

There is no need to relate the grittier details of the appalling clean-up that ensued. Many adult children face the prospect of organizing their parent's homes to prepare for liquidation each year. We found the sad little reminders of the disease that robbed my mother and stepfather of their conscious thought throughout the house: gum wrappers folded very precisely and arranged in a detailed pattern in the guest room; hoarding of old boxes, receipts, and clothing from the early 1960s; stacks of brand new aluminum foil and wax paper and dozens of boxes of cotton balls, yet their toothbrushes were very old; newspapers and magazines amassed in all the closets; and trash everywhere. They had purchased new living room furniture at some point, but because they were afraid to let go of the old, they placed the new pieces directly in front of the worn-out furniture in a stadium seating arrangement. I turned to hire professionals to remove and dispose of tons of metal poles cut to odd lengths, telephone poles purchased to carve Indian totem poles, and damaged window frames with the broken glass still in them, which Bud had kept after he replaced the new windows 15 years before. It took two 20-yard dumpsters, several professional removers, four additional muscular, sweaty guys, two trips of three trucks by the junk man, and weeks and months of bagging trash before the house and garage preparing my parent's home for sale.

From our initial trip to assume guardianship of my parents and their estate to the final sales of the house and land, the entire process took ten months of full-time effort on my part, with Fred's assistance and the aid of others hired in between. It was grueling and painstaking work. I made a point of visiting Mama and Bud every one to two days, and they would look at me plaintively, often in tears, and beg me to take them home. I would hold their hands and try to assure them in some way. I would take them for walks or would try to distract them somehow. During this period, Mama and I slowly became reacquainted. She was still adorable, although more fragile than ever. I do not doubt that she knew of her husband's organic disability and her confusion and deterioration. Suffering from dementia, Alzheimer's, and Parkinson's diseases and never having had the stamina my grandmother was famous for, which I luckily inherited, the illnesses had worn Mama out. Every time I would enter the room they shared, my heart would break.

Throughout this process, I experienced conflicting feelings; one day, I would feel frustration at the ongoing work, and the other, sadness at the state of decline they had evolved to. Occasionally, I would ask myself, 'Why me? What am I doing here?', yet it never occurred to me to not accept responsibility for them or turn away from the enormous job. I had grievances, to be sure, and sometimes, I resented the amount of work involved, the extended interruption in my life, and the disruption for my husband. I often prayed for assistance and the strength to see the project through, then I would get up the next day and start again.

Just as I entered the facility one morning, the staff stopped me to enlist my help. Bud had barred the door to their room and refused to allow the nursing staff to enter for almost 24 hours. Finally, after some time, I persuaded Bud to open the door. The smell immediately assaulted me, but what I saw was even worse. Mama had lost all bodily control and was lying in their shared bed, covered from head to toe in her feces. Bud's Alzheimer's disease manifested as an irritable, hallucinatory paranoia. He was vaguely aware of my mother's predicament but, in his illness, preferred his privacy to her cleanliness and comfort.

I managed to help her stand and cleaned her enough to make it down the hall to the shower. As the warm water touched her face and body, removing the terrible stench, Mama looked up at me and started to cry.

I held her in my arms as she sobbed, the water pouring down her back. Seeing her obvious distress was devastating. No matter what transpired between us, I never wanted my mother to endure this humiliation. Yet, at that moment, the Lord cleansed my heart of the last vestiges of anger and resentment I had harbored. She had suffered enough, and so had I. I told her how much I loved her and told her I forgave her. Mama gripped me tighter, and I stood partially in the shower with her, half-drenched myself. At that moment, I felt the calming presence of the Holy Spirit encircle us. He reached down within my heart, and I felt an expansion in my chest, and I could feel the Holy Spirit absolving me of my sins of resentment and regret. It was the most precious moment of my life.

I can never thank the Lord enough for this gift of service to my mother. During those months, He bestowed upon me His healing grace. Every bag I carried, every frustration I encountered, every heartbreaking court appearance—each day of backbreaking work culminated in a moment of redemption, love, mercy, and kindness I shall never forget.

The Gospel of Mark assures us, 'Therefore, I say to you, all things for which you pray and ask, believe that you have received them, and they will be granted to you.' [The Gospel of Mark 11:24 NASB] Remembering this passage, I prayed for the strength to complete the overwhelming task before me: to grow in faith and to perceive His direct intervention in my life. As always, the Lord answers my prayers though not as I would have anticipated. The Lord often challenges us in ways we may not have expected: St. Paul's struggle with a thorn in his flesh is a good example. As related in Paul's Second Letter to the Corinthians,'..to keep me from exalting myself, there was given to me a thorn in the flesh, a messenger of Satan to Torment - to keep me from exalting myself.' [2 Corinthians 12:4-17 NASB]

The pain must have been debilitating and probably hampering his missionary work, for, as we read, St. Paul pleaded with the Lord three times to remove this hindrance. Yet the Lord refused to ease his suffering, replying to Paul, ' My grace is sufficient for you for my power is made perfect in weakness.' Paul concludes, 'Therefore I delight in weaknesses, in insults, in distresses, in persecutions, in difficulties, in behalf Christ; for when I am weak, then I am strong.' [2 Corinthians 10 NASB]

This passage brought me comfort so many times in my life: my suffering was not pointless. Through the auspices of God's Grace, He entered that painful space with me, knowing there was a purpose and meaning to my suffering, even if that purpose and meaning were unknown to me. God asked me to stir up my faith and employ it faithfully without hinting at the outcome. Jesus promises He will always love us and not forsake us, but He did not promise a walk in the park. Paul's example is ever before us: the Lord instructs us to *activate* our faith: we must continue in daily prayer and worship, knowing that the morning will come in His time and put one foot in front of another to complete the work at hand.

In praying to God a plaintive, *How will I ever get through this?*, the Lord, *who must have planned this all along*, answered my prayer by placing me in the position of caring for my parents daily for an extended period and requiring me to work to keep their care funded by submitting to impending, essential, and needed work with inherent deadlines to be met on a timely basis. The irony of the situation - that I was legally required to spend time with a mother who had betrayed me and legal obligations for her care - was not lost on me. As I completed each challenge, still more challenges lay before me. The days seemed to flow one into another, punctuated by my ever-growing to-do list and visits with Mama, her condition deteriorating. Finally, I realized that my deepest longing - to be free of old hurts and resentments - and my greatest dream - to become more Christ-like - were the *fundamental* goals of this entire situation. I had asked for these blessings repeatedly, and Jesus answered my prayers by enrolling me in the University of Redemption and Discipleship.

Oklahoma, where my parents lived, had enacted stricter guidelines for guardians and trustees: the laws required me to issue written reports periodically and submit regular accountings of all funds and monetary transactions to a judge. After reviewing my latest report, the judge complimented me on my tenure as my parent's guardian and suggested I write a how-to book for other guardians—the Bible verse, 'Well done, good and faithful servant. You were faithful over a few things; I will set you over many things. Enter into the joy of your master!' [Matthew 25:23 NASB] came to mind, and I smiled. Then, as the judge shuffled her papers and signed off on the documents, I whispered a prayer of gratitude to Jesus, whose help, direction, inspiration, and encouragement were instrumental in my completing this onerous duty, much less so expertly.

I had met a task God gave me and felt deserving of His praise and love; I know now that I always was. Before my parents' hospitalization, I accepted a short-term position auditing the accounting department for a parish. Cognizant of the trust inherent in work of this kind, I realized that the Lord had placed in me. He prepared me for the larger, more challenging project with my parents.

This is how the Lord works: He continues to entrust His faithful servants with more of what He values to complete His work here on Earth. Conscious of the importance of my job to the pastor and parish, yet faced with daunting on-the-job resistance from my fellow workers, isolation, and out-right rudeness from exiting members of the department who had completed the work I was examining (which I thought somewhat understandable at the time even if it made it uncomfortable for me), I felt His approval with each day and came to know the 'joy of the master' St. Matthew spoke of.

A few months after the shower incident, I told Mama that Fred and I had to leave Oklahoma for a week to resettle in Florida for Fred's job. Mama and I agreed she would come live with us in Tampa; Bud's behavior had become erratic sometimes, sometimes violent, and we separated them. Fred and I had just arrived in Tampa when two days later, Mama slipped into a coma, and the staff transferred her to the medical hospital. Fred and I came to Florida two days before, but I flew back to Oklahoma City immediately. Although the team kept explaining that she was in a coma and unaware of her surroundings, I begged her nurse to whisper that I was on my way and to ask her to please wait for me. She did.

In her last moments on earth, Mama knew I was there. She would squeeze my hand and turn her head toward my voice. Her face became more placid, the few lines etched upon her porcelain skin seemed to ease, her forehead smooth as satin. As death approached, Mama's stillness, a quiet elegance I had remembered when I was a small child but had not seen for years, returned. Her strange otherworldliness, almost ethereal, not of this earth, began to emerge from its hibernation. I was struck by how beautiful she was, and I realized as I looked at her quiet serenity I was glimpsing the future: *this is how death will be.* And I was reminded of what a teacher she had been to me my entire life: it was she who introduced me to sacred scripture from other cultures and had started me on my quest, introducing me to the joys of reading great books, appreciating music, all forms of artwork; the value of having a goal and achieving it. Yes, she had failed me; at one point, Mama 'dropped her basket,' as Grammy would say, yet she dared to pick herself up and improve her life. She gifted me tremendously, and now she taught me how to die. I will always be grateful to her.

Finally, I was left alone with Mama, holding her hand and whispering that I loved and forgave her until she passed. Mama, shy and retiring, ever fragile, ever lovely and genteel, was a lady, and a lady always knew when to leave.

Chapter 7

SI VIS AMARI AMA

If you want to be loved, love.

IN SINGLING OUT MARY, A very young girl residing in an obscure village during the last years of the reign of Augustus, the first emperor of Rome, God bestowed upon her arguably His greatest honor: to give birth to His Son. As Catholics, we believe the Lord identified Mary from her conception for this role, endowing her with a deep devotion to the Lord, poise, humility, obedience, and dignity. When the angel Gabriel appeared to her to announce God's decision, Mary's immediate acceptance and compliance, her complete surrender to the mighty will of the Holy Spirit, testify to the nobility of her submission. [Luke Chapter 1:38 NASB]. Mary's faithfulness to God, meekness, and devotion would have appealed to Joseph, a scion of the House of David and a man of moral uprightness. We can assume Joseph was an excellent potential marital partner, as the rabbi permitted him to enter a marriage contract with Mary's family. Mary and her family were aware of Joseph's exemplary attributes and illustrated why Mary had agreed to marry Joseph even before her visit from the angel Gabriel.

Reading the Gospel accounts, I am impressed by the events detailed in the account and the more private concerns not included. The harmony of Joseph and Mary's marital relationship is implied.

From the facts, Joseph displayed commendable faith and obedience to God; he protected his little family and loved Jesus as his son. However, Joseph seems to disappear from the story after the incident when Jesus was a young boy, and Mary and Joseph feared they had lost Him in the Temple in Jerusalem. One writer suggested that, as Simeon mentions only Jesus and Mary in his prophecy at the ceremony of Jesus' circumcision, perhaps Simeon was warned that Joseph would not live to see Jesus' three-year ministry and all the events that would unfold.

The Church has endeavored to reveal to the faithful Mary's expanded role in the salvation story; I am also impressed by the Lord's care in choosing Jesus' adoptive father. Throughout the Gospels, Joseph's shining example of a father's sacrificial leadership, work ethic, and faithfulness are clear and had to have had a profound impact on Jesus and Mary. Unlike many widows in first century A.D. Judea, there is no mention of Mary requiring alms from the elders after Joseph leaves the narrative. Jesus started his ministry in his early 30s: one can surmise he focused on providing for the care and sustenance of his mother. I believe if we were to query most Christian believers, they would agree that, even as extraordinary a woman as Mary was, as blessed as Mary is and was, she could not have carried out the Lord's mandate to raise His son without the love, faithfulness, strength and steady hand of Joseph.

Documentation originating in or around the 5th century B.C.E. indicates that ancient Jewish marriages were entered into by couples that grew up together whose fathers, already well-known to one another and usually from similar villages or towns, sought alike families near them so as not to introduce unfamiliar customs to the prospective in-laws. At the time of Jesus' birth, Nazareth was tiny: probably not over 50-100 small families, many related to one another. Customs deemed that a young girl was to be betrothed in early adolescence, probably shortly after the onset of her menses. The groom would be older, often, as assumed in Joseph's case, a full-grown adult.

First-century Jewish marriages recognized and adhered to two different ceremonies, celebrating customs we rarely see today. After the initial ceremony, the betrothal or *erusin,* the groom's father or the groom himself, would pay a *mattan* to the bride, a substantial gift of cash that became the bride's non-refundable endowment. An additional grant of money or valuables, the *mohar,* constituted what they initially thought of as an actual purchase price for the bride. This practice continued through the centuries. However, by the first century A.D., the value of the items given by the groom's family to the bride became representative of the bride's importance to her prospective in-laws. Our modern eyes are raised askance at the notion of a 'purchase price' for a bride; however, in the balance sheet of familial finances and relations, although men or sons provided income, daughters or female relations carried a significant value domestically. Therefore, the bride's 'equity' would increase the overall domestic value assumed by the groom and his family, creating a loss of that same "domestic equity" value to the bride's parents. The *mohar* compensated the bride's family for the loss. At about the same time as the *mohar*, the groom's family gifted the bride a more personal - and expensive - item meant to set her apart in the family, elevating her status from chattel to valued partner. The groom's family also presented the bride's mother and brothers gifts of precious jewelry or other more minor but valuable offerings, which the bride's family also kept.

The bride's father hosted the second ceremony, the *nissuin* or marriage, constituting his sole obligation and expense. It was within his purview to host either a lavish nuptial party or a smaller wedding celebration. Whatever embellishments the bride's father chose to include, custom demanded that the wedding celebration last seven days but expected little else of the bride's family. The couple would cohabitate after the seven days of celebration had concluded.

During this betrothal period, they also included signing a marriage contract by the groom, known as a *ketubah*. Dating from the ancient period before the first destruction of the Temple in Jerusalem, the *ketubah*, initially written in Aramaic, is the vernacular spoken by the ordinary Jewish people of the time (it is believed that Jesus spoke in Aramaic) and states the explicit rights of the bride and upon what conditions she agrees to marry the groom. The *ketubah* became more critical after the destruction of the Temple in 587 BC and the subsequent scattering of the Twelve Tribes by the Babylonians. Known as the *diaspora,* the Babylonians, having conquered the Jewish kingdoms, cruelly uprooted the Jewish people, sending them to the far corners of their enormous empire with very little of their personal property. The upheaval and loss of property seem to have influenced later versions of the *ketubah*. The document clearly states that the *mohar* and *mattan* are remittable by the groom and his family to the bride and kept by her should the groom die or initiate a divorce.

The Gospels clearly state that when the angel appeared to Mary, Joseph, and Mary were betrothed, we must apply these same recognized obligations and ceremonials in their union. We, therefore, can assume that the initial *erusin* ceremony had already taken place, the terms of the *ketubah* had been, or were being, agreed upon and signed by Joseph, and that he would remit the *mohar* and *mattan* fees to Saint Anne and Saint Joachim, Mary's parents, in compensation for losing their daughter.

Mary's admission to Joseph of her pregnancy must have stunned him; this was a girl he and his family had known all her life. He must have felt deeply betrayed by her and her family. Nevertheless, after he had time to consider, as stated in the Gospels, Joseph planned to follow through with his marriage to Mary anyway, to protect her and to avoid her suffering the discredit and humiliation of a first-century unmarried, pregnant girl. He must have also realized that had the truth been known, their betrothal meant public accusation, followed by a devastating Rabbinic trial on charges of adultery, a capital crime for Judean women—the punishment: death by stoning. Joseph's decision also meant Mary's parents' expensive outlay of funds to underwrite the cost of the seven-day wedding feast for a marriage that would not last long.

Additional circumstances might have also weighed heavily upon Joseph: Mary's explanation for how she fell pregnant may have sounded suspect to Joseph. The Nazareth of Jospeh's time was a small village of little consequence, located north of Jerusalem. Situated approximately four miles from a district office of the Roman military in Sepphoris and just over the border of Samaria and Galilee, Nazareth must have hosted the travelers, Jewish, gentile, Samaritan or Arab, as well as Roman soldiers progressing to or from Gaza, or Sepphoris, even onto Herod's royal seat in Caesarea Philippi. Unwanted pregnancies amongst the local populace were a known by-product of military outposts. His wrestling with all the circumstances and determination not to expose Mary speaks to Joseph's extraordinary kindness. Even if he had considered that Mary may have had relations with someone not of their faith, a far more egregious act of adultery, Joseph's shielding of Mary also speaks to his character. He would not subject her to, at the very least, ridicule. These additional facts more fully illustrate Joseph's extraordinary tenderness and sensitivity, which may not have been known or understood. We must also consider the prevalence of both early and late-term abortion in Roman culture, as well as the discarding of unwanted live births. Although this practice may not have been common in the Jewish culture, Mary's family, nestled a mere four miles from a large administrative and military center of the Roman government, with government personnel of all kinds stationed far from home and the subjugation of the Jewish populace, must have been well aware of the unwanted pregnancies that occurred at least a few times, and, when faced with stoning, a dangerous situation possibly solved as Romans commonly did in the capital by abortion or the discarding of live birth. Finally, given what we now know about the costs of the *erusin, mohar,* and *mattan* paid by the groom, Joseph's kindness and generosity are profound as a carpenter with limited resources.

I shall never forget the incredible moment when I read about the first-century ceremonials and realized how special Joseph was: this is the first in a long line of successive occasions when this humble carpenter steps into the salvation story to become a courageous leader. Quiet, industrious, and pious, Joseph is one of the great superheroes of the New Testament and the salvation story.

Although the circumstances of Mary's family of origin were very humble, as Mary herself admitted herself [Luke 1:47-48 NASB], Joseph established himself sufficiently enough in his chosen profession that the rabbi felt he could assume the responsibilities of a family. Later, after Gabriel acquaints Joseph with the facts surrounding Mary's pregnancy in a dream, his faith is such that he accepts the truth as the angel relates it to him and never questions it. [Matthew 1:20 N.I.V.]

Mary and her parents made an excellent choice. Listed below are some of the character traits credited to St. Joseph the Worker, embodying many of the necessary attributes every intelligent woman should look for in a mate:

* Responsible, faithful, and humble: St. Joseph was faithful to Mary and an obedient servant of God
* Placed his vocation as a protective husband and father above his professional life: Joseph abandoned from established carpentry

business to hide Mary and baby Jesus safely, avoiding King Herod's 'Massacre of the Innocents' before traveling on to Egypt, to live in obscurity for two years.

* Joseph supported Jesus' ministry and destiny: Although he may not have lived to see Jesus' ministry, Joseph knew of his adopted son's future from Mary and Gabriel; he witnessed this boy's exceptional learning and insight as Jesus discussed scripture with elders at the Temple when Jesus was a small boy. Jesus showed knowledge and erudition far more in-depth than his parents could have provided, and Joseph must have recognized it. He protected the boy and loved him; in doing so, he defended the founding of the Church and the salvation of mankind.

* Joseph's willingness to live a celibate life: as Catholics, we recognize their union's profound sanctity in their commitment to celibacy.

Why include this extensive - albeit interesting! - analysis of the marriage customs of first-century Israelites and St. Joseph's virtues? To illustrate the integral role faith, family, and values played in their important choices, especially in selecting a mate. They lived with a high degree of intentionality in accordance with the Laws of Moses. The Mosaic Law provided guidance and a framework for how they should live. Most ancient Israelites worked on small farms or in craft and trade-related positions, unlike the *goyim*, who were employed in various professions, such as merchants, politicians, careers, and civil services, with only a minority of Roman citizens working in farming and the trades. Within Jewish culture, everyone expected to work diligently until the Sabbath. Boys would assume an apprenticeship with a local tradesman as arranged by their family after their Bar Mitzvah at age 13. The young man's family would also play the most crucial role in choosing his wife. Given the property and monetary stakes in selecting a spouse, the parent's input and approval were essential. This pre-eminence of worship and family in the daily lives of St. Joseph and his contemporaries also speaks to their faith formation. Sundown in first-century Judea did not include T.V. and board games. Often, the men would read scripture aloud to their families, modeling the importance of daily worship to their children and preparing them to be parents to their offspring. Again, they emphasize faith, worship, and hard work daily. The Lord deemed the Jews as the chosen people to illustrate to the world how we are to live, their lives defined by *purpose*.

In one of my late-night Google searches, I came across one of the best summations of Talmudic wisdom I have ever read: The Talmudic Formula. Featured in the Jewish journal Aish.com and written by Bob Deiner, a hugely successful entrepreneur, lawyer, and hedge fund manager.

In his epic tome, *Summa Theologica*, St. Thomas Aquinas speaks of the virtues God endows us. In a different edition, also written by Aquinas, is a commentary on his *Summa* as well as works by Peter Abelard, Aristotle, and specifically Peter Lombard, *Scriptum super libros Sententiarum* in which he delineates very specifically the virtues, assigning each to one of two groups:

- The Natural Virtues: Also referred to as the *Cardinal Virtues* (CCC 1804); cardinal because they precede the second group and are endowed to us at birth, much like the *Natural Law* (CCC 1954; Romans 1:18-32 ESV). They are justice, prudence, temperance, and fortitude.
- The Theological Virtues: The virtues relate specifically to God, are elevated from those endowed at birth, and are an inchoation from God (*'inchoatia virtutum a Deo*). They are faith, hope, and love or charity.

Ultimately, the reliance upon all of these virtues is the origin of our true happiness. By true happiness, I refer to the definition suggested by Aristotle, which is the ultimate goal of human life. Aristotle defines happiness not as a feeling but as the habit of living virtuously: 'He is happy who lives in accordance with complete virtue and is sufficiently equipped with external goods, not for some chance period but throughout a complete life.' (*Nicomachean Ethics, 1101a10*)

Developing a good character through applying the virtues requires consistency in doing the right thing, even in difficult situations. My beloved Grammy explained it best: 'The things of God are usually difficult in the beginning and easy in the end. Likewise, the things that are not of God are usually easy in the beginning and difficult in the end.' As we can see, this axiom applies to any situation. For example, Aristotle believed that financial stability was a significant area of derived human happiness. When cruising the Black Friday sales on an overcast day, it is much easier to cheer me up by whipping out my credit card and buying those leggings I've had my eye on that just went on sale. But in the long run, that purchase becomes just another credit card debt racking up interest every month. The same is true for eating chocolate cake, ignoring projects around the house, or snapping at my husband: the long-term correction is far more complex than the momentary exercise of temperance. Grammy was a genius.

Jesus gives us another clue to happiness with his succinct Great Commandments: *You shall love God with all your heart, and with all your soul, and with all of your mind. The second is like unto it, for you shall love your neighbor as yourself.* In His directive, Jesus says nothing about *happiness*; yet He is unequivocal about our *purpose* and how we are to live. C. S. Lewis states it unequivocally in his book *Mere Christianity*, 'I'm not really sure if God cares if we [feel] happy; He wants us to love and be loved.' The Lord created us out of love and sent us here to learn to love and to be loved. He sent us here to be perfected by learning how to love and sacrifice for that love so that we may return to Him, which He longs for. And if we are honest with ourselves, so do we.

Unfortunately, although endowed at birth with natural virtues, we are yet laden with concupiscence, the sinful nature we inherited from Adam and Eve, burdening modern life's daily choices and temptations and sometimes overwhelming us. By further bestowing faith, hope, and love through baptism, the Lord empowers us with virtues that can subdue our fallen nature and draw us closer to Him. How do we grow in these virtues? By trusting in God and employing these virtues in our communion with Him and His children. The apostle Paul provides the simple steps to follow:

> 'Rejoice in the Lord always. I will say it again: Rejoice! Let your heart's gentleness be evident to all. The Lord is near. Do not be anxious about anything, but in every situation, by prayer and petition, with thanksgiving, present your requests to God. And the peace of God, which transcends all understanding, will guard your hearts and your minds in Christ Jesus.' [Philippians 4:4-7 NIV]

St. Paul further states in his Letter to the Romans: that the mastery of our feelings and actions will lead us to

> God and,' May God, the source of hope, fill you with joy and peace through your faith in Him. Then you will overflow with hope.' [Romans 15:13 God's Word Translation]

Yet, how do we know we truly trust God to meet our deepest longings and needs?

Although I met my husband Fred at work – he was the C.E.O./founder of the company I worked for - we were work colleagues for three years, until after he sold his company. Within the context of day-to-day operations, and then later, when he sold the company to a larger competitor, I had a bird's eye view of his decision-making in terms of the structure of the sale of the company for the benefit of the investors, as well as the way he protected the employee's health care insurance, 401k, and accrued vacation time through the transaction process. After the sale, we started dating. He met my grown daughter and her two boys, still toddlers. As Fred had no children, I was unsure how he would respond; he treated us all to a zoo trip and had both boys on his shoulders within a few minutes, peering at orangutans. As the relationship progressed, Fred was open about his plans for the future and what he wanted from life. He admitted he had some residual issues to work through from his divorce, and we worked through much of this by dating for four years before we married. Throughout this period, Fred made his intentions toward me known. Given his stature in the business community, Fred's reputation for honesty and forthright business dealings was well-known, adding to my confidence in him. He was open with me about the terms of his divorce, and I found him beyond fair to his ex-wife in their settlement. As we grew closer, I had the comfort of evaluating Fred as a potential partner and concluded this was an honorable, faithful, and kind man I could trust. My faith was well placed.

As I write this chapter, it is a week before our anniversary, and I find myself awake at two in the morning, stewing over a heart-to-heart Fred and I had earlier that day. At first, we argued, then discussed the current issue, which stems from an ongoing problem that has been a source of friction between us for years. The pattern has always been that if I ask Fred to complete a chore, he will agree to do it and promptly forget. When I remind him, the pattern repeats: Fred nods in agreement and promptly forgets again. I usually respond one of two ways: my first reaction would be to sigh, grumble a few words, and complete the chore myself. The second would be to become annoyed and confront him. He would respond by lashing out in his defense, and then a fight ensues, culminating in a two-day standoff: me raising my voice periodically and Fred sulking in the guest bedroom.

After ten years of this pattern, choosing either response didn't get me closer to what I wanted or the chores completed consistently. Ultimately, I realized that Fred would never change. So, I accepted full responsibility for the household chores, financial management, planning, and errands—our day-to-day life, option #3. However, by doing everything myself, I never got what I wanted as I hadn't accepted all of this responsibility from a place of peace. Instead, I was angry and resentful. *It was not fair.*

As I mentioned, Fred and I met at work: he was the founder and C.E.O. of a $250 million finance company. Nationally recognized for his entrepreneurship and innovative approaches, Fred's firm employed approximately two hundred people nationwide. Years later, when Fred agreed to sell the company, he notified all the employees of the sale, and I, like everyone else, began the search for a new position. Although I worked just down the hall in the administrative area, Fred kept to himself, and we rarely spoke. Frankly, we were not too fond of one another: I found him aloof and arrogant, interacting only with the most senior employees. On the other hand, he, the unhappy recipient of some of my emails, was bursting with helpful hints for increased efficiency and ways to save money on expenses. Although he followed several of my suggestions, he thought I was an officious pest.

So I was surprised when he approached me about staying on as part of the transition team. He explained that a purchase of this kind requires up to six months to transition departments smoothly, and we to ensure that it didn't inconvenience our customers. Accepting his proposal would extend my employment and allow me more time to secure a permanent position. I accepted. Several larger departments had started transitioning by the second month, and the staff dwindled quickly. Fred and I worked closely, following up on details and planning the next handoff phase.

The new company assumed more departments approximately four months later; the movement of departments reduced the staff by 75%. Daily, Fred and I huddled with just a few folks, ancillary staff, in and out throughout the day. At lunchtime, this core group of senior staff chose a local joint to grab a burger, which Fred often treated. In the last thirty days of operations, all the employees were gone, and my friend had accepted another position as H.R. director, leaving Fred and me alone all day. By midday, we began the daily search for new places to eat, and on Fridays, cutting out a little early for happy hour. We discovered that we had more in common than we knew: both of us nerdy types that love to be holed up in the library's history section sipping coffee and reading about long-dead English monarchs. The night of the last day, we toured the building one last time, and as he handed me the keys to forward to the new owners, Fred asked if I wanted to have dinner. By the end of the evening, we were a couple, and we have been together ever since. Fred and I have been together for 19 years.

During a recent heart-to-heart conversation, Fred and I shared some of the pain we still felt from our respective divorces; he acknowledged that, in the first year of our marriage, he hadn't been as committed to our wedding as he was now and that this lack of commitment was about his fears and not a deficiency within me.

And he was not alone: I had brought my pain and fears into the situation, exacerbated by my memories of childhood abuse. As opposites, when faced with triggering concerns, Fred would overreact and become tentative and emotionally removed; I would overreact to his overreaction, cling tighter, and try harder. I spared no effort to garner assurances against what I feared was my inevitable abandonment: either go out of my way to please him or criticize him for not loving me. So Fred's admission and realization came as no surprise to me. Hearing the words spoken was like a distant bell ringing in the background, a sound I had listened to my entire life; *he will abandon you…ding…he doesn't love you…ding ding.*

Why do I continue to rely upon my flawed thinking? Reflecting upon the various terrible decisions that led to many of the tragedies recorded in both the New and Old Testaments, it is clear that human beings consistently rely upon the flaws in our character that created the misunderstanding. We think we know what is best for us, clinging to our dogged self-determination to carve our path, often in direct violation of some decree from God instructing us to avoid the very action we intend to do.

Our greatest mistakes are born of our best intentions: we want to help and fix them for a loved one; we know what they should do. So our first inclination is to offer money, help, or our favorite gift to others: unsolicited advice. Despite their repeated spurnings of our timely counsel and wise words, we inevitably proffer hasty solutions that we are sure are just what the person needs to hear. And then we suffer for it. Why do we do this? Despite our missteps, many of which the hapless recipient of our unsolicited advice is well aware of, we genuinely believe we know what's best.

So it was with Fred. I increased the injury to my husband's tender feelings by providing him with the insight I just knew he would appreciate at that moment," Well, you feel that way because….." Big mistake. Fred's face fell. He turned and walked away from me mid-sentence. The ensuing silence was deafening. I had successfully communicated to my husband that he was a) at fault, b) broken; and see c)too incompetent to solve this problem himself. Really. Big. Mistake.

As I pondered our conversations, I recalled a Bible verse, *'And we know that God causes all things to work together for good to those who love God, to those who are called according to His purpose'* [Romans 8:28 NASB]. I realized that during this entire situation with Fred - his fear and reluctance to commit emotionally to our marriage and subsequent admission, my disappointment, hurt, and anger - God permitted us to experience that we might see the dysfunction in our behavior and relationship and turn to our Father for help. The Holy Spirit reminded me of the words of C. S. Lewis, 'God whispers to us in our pleasure, speaks in our conscience, but shouts in our pains: it is his megaphone to rouse a deaf world.'

With that came the realization that he should carry more of the household workload. He wanted to be my husband, head of the household, and leader of our family, and he was willing to start helping me without being reminded and asking me for suggestions. I related the feeling of disrespect in having to either repeat the request or remind him constantly— that he seemed to tune me out or refuse to take the initiative around the house. So, in response to his offer, I told him that whatever he was willing to do would be appreciated. I proposed a daily list that we formulated together; the list would be left in our home office and could be viewed by both of us throughout the day. We agreed that, except for preparing dinner and washing up the dishes.

Great, perfect. I finally have a husband, partner, and help-mate willing to share the load. *So why did I still feel resentful? Shouldn't I have felt relieved?* Instead, I heard that discouraging voice, which sounded like my mother, whisper, *It won't last; Fred will not see this through for long.* So, there I was, sleepless at 2 in the morning. I sat up and looked around the room; my Bible was beside me. *I won't look at it; I want to be mad now. It's just not fair.* And then I heard myself say, *'I want to be mad now.'* Why would anyone in their right mind *want* to be mad? I remembered what Fred would tell me in the heat of a disagreement when we had reached an impasse, "You just want to be mad at me." *He was right.*

The realization of how selfish I acted seemed to slowly well within me, much like the sun rising in the East: realization gradually extended its tentacles of light along the mountain tops of my mind, illuminating a few dark valleys of resentment lurking below. In those valleys, I found my Hurt Pocket, that remote repository of painful memories, disappointments, criticisms, and, in my case, verbal, physical, and sexual abuse.

As I mentioned, I underwent the annulment process as part of my conversion to the Catholic church. As a result, an in-depth, extensive questionnaire about my history, covering my birth, family of origin, marriage, and divorce, was a mandatory exercise that took me a week to complete. Although the questions did ask me about my spouse, over half the questions inquired about my response to his behavior and how I felt, thought, and acted before, during, and after each event. As embarrassing as some of the questions were to answer, the queries as to my faith and relationship with God were perhaps the most surprising: I heard later that the Tribunal had encountered quite a few people who had been through childhood abuse and had turned to God, but very few had spent 20 years reading sacred scripture of a variety of faiths and prayed to God as I understood Him at each step. Extremely personal and invasive, the priest I worked with prepped me for this exercise by explaining that the more truthful I was, the easier it would be for the Tribunal to determine how consciously I had chosen my partner and what other factors weighed upon me at the time I married, including, and especially, my faith.

I thought about this over the next few hours, alone in our bedroom while my husband and two dogs lay fast asleep in other beds. Finally, through much prayer and journaling, the light of recognition made everything clear: I had been resenting Fred for not appreciating all the sacrifices I had made on his behalf. And then it dawned on me: *he never asked me to. The sacrifices I had made for Fred were choices I had made freely.*

And hadn't he sacrificed for me? As a middle-aged divorced man with no children of his own, Fred accepted my grown daughter as his child and her boys as his grandsons. He loves them, cares for them, assists them financially, and involves himself in their lives. Fred is tender-hearted and consistently provides my daughter Taryn with love, support, and advice if she is going through something. He has forged a father-daughter bond with her that they both cherish.

So who is the selfish one here? Who is not loving who? Which of us needs to re-commit to the marriage? I realized that it was me. Years ago, before I met Fred, I had prayed, *Father, I want a sacrificial leader as a husband and father.* Feeling the tears in my eyes, I realized that the Lord had granted my prayer. At that moment, tears spilling down my cheeks, I spoke words of praise and thanksgiving to God for my wonderful husband.

Many of you who carry the deep heartbreak of divorce may relate to the feeling of homelessness I experienced for years, of my home ripped away. Given the broken bonds of my childhood, that sadness of not feeling at home, no matter where I lived, would engulf me. I am a very determined, directed, and disciplined person. God blessed me with the fortitude to keep going during difficult circumstances and never give up. I did my best to raise my daughter and worked hard to keep her safe. The frantic schedule of a working mother kept me on the move constantly; I had very little time during her formative years to contemplate the sorrow of not *belonging*. When my daughter grew up and moved out with friends, I experienced a profound loss, feeling the weight of my aloneness.

What I have also come to realize is that I am not alone in these feelings. My husband's avoidant coping style, seemingly impervious to what is happening around him, also fell prey to these apprehensions. *As a result, he also suffered deep heartbreak from his divorce.*

Marriage challenges us each to serve our spouse sacrificially. As a married fisherman, St. Peter possessed first-hand experience in relationships and is particularly insightful and instructive on this point, admonishing wives, "Your adornment should not be an external one … but rather the hidden character of the heart, expressed in the imperishable beauty of a gentle and calm disposition, which is precious in the sight of God. For this is also how the holy women who hoped in God once sued to adorn themselves" (First Peter 3:3-5 N.A.B.). He goes on to say that when it comes to the Lord's commandments, "even if some [husbands] disobey the word, they may be won over without a word by their wives' conduct when they observe your reverent and chaste behavior" (First Peter 3:1-2 N.A.B.). In her landmark book, *The Resolution for Women*, Priscilla Shirer references these Petrine admonitions and further notes, "If we will funnel our wifely behavior and responses through this biblical filter, we will intentionally become more careful and circumspect."

Ultimately Jesus chose this very flawed, married fisherman to be one of His greatest apostles, the rock of the church, and the first pope. Reading his letters, I appreciate Jesus's inspired choice. St. Peter did not limit his admonishment to wives alone; he also reminded the husbands 'to live with your wives in understanding showing honor to the weaker female sex, since we are joint heirs of the gift of life, so that your prayers will not be hindered' (1Peter 3:7 NAB). I doubt that many husbands correlate impatient, dismissive behaviors towards their wives as impacting the outcome of their greatest dreams and aspirations for themselves and their future or that they may be unwittingly subverting their best-laid plans by unloving behavior towards their wives.

Interestingly, in his letter to the Ephesians, St. Paul, an unmarried rabbi, challenges both partners in very distinctive ways, confronting weaknesses inherent in both of the sexes, when he states, "In any case, each one of you should love his wife as himself, and the wife should respect her husband." In this passage, St. Paul calls upon the partners to tackle the area most difficult for each; husbands, if they are like mine and many of my friend's spouses, for better or worse, may typically cope with the world non-verbally, bracing themselves in silence, *alone*. When my husband holds up his phone after work to surf the internet, he signals *I need silent downtime now*. His instinct isn't always to communicate his daily concerns, so it is challenging to approach me and extend himself consciously. I am typically far more verbal towards him and will interrupt his downtime and demand a decision about something I've been sitting on all day. These blurtings and interruptions feel disrespectful to him. While I communicate a temporary frustration meant for a particular, transient incident, Fred often interprets these complaints as my unhappiness with *him* and feels disrespected and offended. He doesn't hear how I feel hurt by his being excluded or unloved, and I fail to explicitly state the underlying feelings pressing upon my heart. When Fred suddenly changes his approach, resets the sails, and reaches for me when I am frustrated, I initially resist but then feel his strong arms around me, and my head hits that big chest, and I feel better. Nothing in this world makes me happier.

All things are possible with God, and when I am willing to listen to His voice, ever patient, ever instructive, when I choose to look past the present circumstances and see the larger picture in the light of Jesus' greatest commandment, that we love one another, I see all the ways the Lord has healed both Fred and I. Steel, that most potent of metals, signifies the 11th wedding anniversary. How perfect that I should come to this realization today. Steel is a synthesis of iron and carbon placed in extreme heat. I know I am the iron: strong yet incredibly flawed, I have been perfected by the Lord's application of heat in the presence of Fred's carbon, a dynamic mineral taking the form of coal amongst other forms, and that, in the presence of heat, brings out the best in what it is exposed to and is the very essence of what is strongest and most precious in our world: diamonds. Fred and I have faced various adversities, many by friends and partners and some quite devastating. Yet, we have been synthesized together, heated by circumstances into a new substance, steel. The Lord works in mysterious ways.

I have made amends to my husband for my slights against him, and I know he forgives me. But the lesson didn't end there. So I have a new prayer to offer the Lord: *Father, make me into the wife this wonderful man deserves.*

Chapter 8
THE QUEST

When you look for me, you will find me. Yes, when you seek me with all of your heart.

JEREMIAH 29:13 NCB

*T*HE EDITORS AT MERRIAM-WEBSTER DEFINE a *quest* as an 'investigation; an act of seeking; a person who searches or makes inquiries,' characterizing it as, 'He (who) refuses to give up his quest for the truth.' A truer word was never spoken.

While I have photos of our family dressed in our Sunday best to attend my father's favorite Southern Baptist Church, I don't recall the services themselves. I have no memories of any faith instruction from anyone. Before my parents were married, Mama attended Biola College, at its original location in downtown Los Angeles, and belonged to a strict Baptist community that prohibited dancing and drinking alcohol and discouraged parties, as most people know them. Daddy's church was on the streets. A high school dropout, he escaped the rough and tumble life of the mean streets in Richmond, California, by joining the merchant marines. When they married, Daddy suggested they join a Southern Baptist congregation, a bit racy for Mama, but she went.

Unfortunately, their affiliation with the Southern Baptist faith, or any other organized religion, was short-lived. I suppose they must have been laboring under a kind of spiritual dissonance - a conscious or unconscious struggle between their outward beliefs versus the unspoken behaviors and shameful secrets in our home, rendering their weekly treks to church more and more unbearable. They fell away from their faith community long before I was aware of its absence, and thus I grew up untrained and unfamiliar with Christianity's precepts. Watching Charlton Heston strike a stone with his staff and fear in the heart of Yul Brynner's pharaoh, then holding up the stone tablets, was the full extent of my Biblical formation.

Through every fault of his own, my father was incarcerated for fraud and tax evasion during my last two years of high school. As a result of ruining our family financially, the federal government seized our assets and garnished Mama's paycheck to repay the debt and make reparations to the injured parties. We each reacted differently to this disastrous situation: I turned even further inward, hiding in the library at school, too ashamed to show my face, uninterested in my school work. On the other hand, my mother turned to God and became acquainted with nearby Religious Science church members. Her initial reading of the church's textbook and insistence upon my accompanying her to Sunday services first piqued my curiosity. Although I made a point of rolling my eyes and groaning as only a teenage girl can do, I did recognize the positive effect all the reading, prayer, and church attendance had upon my mother and me. Reading the textbook, repeating the encouraging prayers and affirmations, and attending the services were calming.

In reading the textbook, I found some of it confusing; Mama explained to me that her new-found faith was 'metaphysical.' She went on to clarify that the Religious Science Church recognizes the wisdom, but not the divinity, of Jesus and denies the existence of Satan and Hell. Religious scientists, she said, view Jesus as the most enlightened of the Great Teachers, much like Buddha and Confucius, but not the only one. She studied the ancient Gnostics and read the Dead Sea Scrolls voraciously. While I did not understand many of the concepts, I, too, was intrigued: as her library of sacred text grew, I took advantage of her investment and began studying. Our independent study became a shared endeavor; Mama, far more advanced than I (she studied Ancient Greek in college and could translate primary sources), directed me toward books correlating to her new-found beliefs.

After studying for several months, Mama's complete shift from her

Baptist beliefs seemed full: she began to deny the presence of evil in the world and the existence of Satan, taking a very dim view of most organized religions, the Catholics specifically, relegating their Roman rites to superstition, her opinion immutable: one was either with God as she understood Him or out of His presence. Although I had followed Mama in lockstep for several months, this statement alarmed me, and my instincts told me she might be off base in her assertions.

Still, my life did begin to change over that last summer of high school: I was happier, and I lost weight. I even started to exercise, bike riding around the neighborhood and swimming laps in our pool. When school reconvened that September, I made friends with girls I barely knew, engaging in conversations and easy banter. Later, they invited me to join a popular off-campus girls club, and I accepted. My concentration at school also improved - my senior year report cards were all A's and B's. I began to see the connection between God and happiness, and I realized there was something to this and wanted to learn more. As I ventured out on my quest, I was grateful to my mother's advanced studies and exceptional library: she encouraged my reading and exploration; indeed, her scholarship and erudition stand out as characteristics I hope I have inherited.

My quest through ancient scripture, history, and early cultures had many starts and stops and began in earnest later in my 20s after the birth of my daughter, a challenging health problem, and the failure of my marriage. My daughter split her time each week between her two parents, leaving me evenings at home alone. I spent many an early evening in the library or combing the shelves of used bookstores, endlessly searching for 'the truth' – why I was born, why my life evolved as it did. Finally, I felt sure there was meaning and purpose behind the events that had taken place.

This example illustrated a truism often repeated in my life and my formation as a Christian woman: Human beings are multi-faceted. There are no white hats or black hats. Even the most pious Christian is capable of pernicious envy and appalling criticism and judgment of their fellow man. Every human possesses a fallen nature and is therefore capable of both good and evil, yet, by the grace of God, forever also carries within them the light of Christ. However, we Christians often fail to perceive that light or to believe it is present in our fellow men. No matter how much we fail one another, God sees the light of Christ He placed within us even when we cannot. To follow Jesus is to be *inclusive*, forgive, and try again. Satan the Liar whispers words of discord, disdain, judgment, and separation. Holy Spirit fosters *communion* with the Trinity and one another in all things.

For me, in reading history, I did not limit my focus to the shaping of governments, the movement of armies, or the meaningful strides in human development; diving into the chronicles of antiquity to our present-day exposed me to other peoples' cultures and to the gods they believed in. And I found that, for each characteristic that appeared to differentiate groups of people, there were also threads of similarity in which they were united. Affirmed by recognizing these similarities in all peoples, I endeavored to find God for myself. My search for my creator came from an intrinsic need to determine my true identity and understand and commune with Him. My desire to know God led me to commune with my fellow man. Determined to learn more about different people, I would focus on our similarities and differences to train my mind to perceive others differently than my parents.

The return to love, real love, healing, and transformation, was a years-long quest for God that led me through some of humanity's most beautiful tributes to divinity and the sacred texts of a few of the world's great religions. Despite the various cultural influences, particular themes repeatedly emerged: a higher power created and governs the universe; this higher power is a universal intelligence possessing infinite mind capabilities and infinite mercy. My journey led me through some of the most inspiring words of wisdom humanity has ever recorded. Although I provide just three examples here, I found the liturgy of each faith at once soulful, lyrical, and life-sustaining.

BUDDHA

When I first approached a Buddhist Dharma center, I found the rituals, chanting, emphasis on detachment from the material, and respect for all of life very appealing. Moreover, the monks were never put off by the endless questions posed by a curious neophyte: I found them willing to share as time allowed and patient with every question I posited. And if they didn't have an immediate answer for me, they charmingly admitted that there were many answers they didn't know. So rarely do we encounter someone who admits they don't have an answer in our Western culture. So rarely still are those moments we are willing to accept this to ourselves.

The Buddhist eschews attachment to the material, as he believes it is in the grasping for the material that lies at the root of all human suffering. Initially developed in small villages before literacy, much like the Hebrews and their early oral traditions eventually coded in the Mishnah, Buddhism relied for centuries upon oral tradition. Buddha represented his Four Noble Truths in a straightforward, practical way that appealed to the villager's intelligence, common sense, instinct, and conscience. Buddhism does not aspire to lofty heights or the center stage; ceremonials are at a minimum: one may desire to follow Buddha, then follows him by adhering to a silent pledge the believer makes within themselves. It is a pearl of transcendental wisdom, your journey, or spiritual awakening.

The *Four Noble Truths include*:

1. Life means suffering
2. The origin of suffering is the attachment to the material
3. It is possible to end suffering through resisting desire, renouncing violence and cruelty, and employing compassion for all living things
4. The Noble Eight-Fold path: keeping the four noble truths always uppermost as well as the right intention, in speech, in actions, in your livelihood, in your effort, in mindfulness, and in meditation

Buddhism's teaching of non-attachment to the material was refreshing and peaceful. Reading and studying Eastern religions, I recognized the disconnection between my thoughts and reality. Buddha was instrumental in helping me to identify the root of my unhappiness: I was inhibiting the expression of my life and its purpose with my thoughts.

There is a ready acceptance of new believers in the communities; when you arrive, it is as though they expect to meet you. I found a refreshing respect for the individual and a recognition that we are all on the same path to the same destination, traveling on our way in our own time.

One of the more enduring lessons I learned from Buddha was a confirmation of what I had begun to suspect: suffering inhabits all earthly life. Although this life brings much enjoyment and delight, one must *expect* to suffer. We measure our short life span on this lovely planet by the amount of tribulation we traverse, like crossing a low-lying bridge over stormy seas, menacing white caps rising to the surface, daring us to fall. I had suffered terribly, *yet I found that only by giving the love I never received was my pain finally assuaged.* I recognized my true purpose, the very reason I was born, was to worship my Creator to carry out His mission on Earth to help others also suffering, and in so doing, glorify the very force that created me. The only way to accomplish this goal was to extend myself beyond where I was comfortable. In meditation, I recognized that I had become comfortable in my resentment and judgment of the parents that had wronged me; of school officials that declined to report what was happening in my home, although they witnessed injuries confirming what they must have suspected; and of the physician who turned a blind eye. I had grown used to my pity pot: it was warm and cozy. I would stoke the burning embers of my bitterness, keeping my self-righteous furor alive and well. Buddha helped me recognize these negative attachments and understand the pain I felt detaching from them. Over time, I realized that the wheel of human suffering would continue until we each accepted the truth: only compassion can end the anguish.

Another aspect of my journey through Buddhism was recognizing – and accepting – who I truly am and my limitations. Not all doors were open, and I could not succeed alone. However, Buddhism helped me recognize the connectedness all creatures share and their inherent divinity. I began to realize the light of God all around me.

During this study period, I worked on a detox unit as a psychiatric nurse with alcoholics. After just a few months, I started to recognize a few of the same faces turning up in our lobby. When they were admitted to the locked unit to dry out, I would ask them how they arrived at our door again. Over and over, many of the patients would reply, 'My best thinking got me here.'

As an adult, I recognized that the events I experienced as a child hampered my overall judgment. As a result, my discernment was inherently flawed; I did not view the world as it truly is. Many of the women I encountered at work, suffering from alcoholism and drug addiction, had endured a similar childhood to mine: I can recall a young girl who had been severely beaten but was so high on angel dust she didn't feel the bruises, relating later on, after her detox, of her sexual assault at the hand of a family friend. Sitting in the group therapy session, listening to her share her story, I silently thanked the Lord for His blessings in my life: He had placed a light within me that prevented me from falling into drug abuse, alcoholism, or prostitution; before I knew it was Him, Jesus blessed me with the Holy Spirit to light my way.

As I reflect on my time with Buddha, I recall the charming story of Prince Siddhartha:

Prince Siddhartha Gautma was born in the 6th century BC in Nepal, the oldest son of the king of Shakyas, a small province known for its poverty. Raised in luxury and splendor within the palace walls, his father kept him isolated from human miseries and suffering and discouraged the prince from venturing out amongst his people. Married at 16 to a beautiful princess, Siddhartha continued his luxurious isolation for another 13 years, raising his family within the safety of the royal fortress.

One day his curiosity to know what lay beyond the fortifications prompted him to escape, and he snuck out the gates with only one servant to attend to him. Siddhartha was immediately confronted with the realities of human frailty: he encountered the aged, and his servant explained that humans grow old. Next, he witnessed diseased men and women dying in the streets, the alleyways littered with decaying corpses; his servant explained human death. The prince then observed a naked ascetic starving; his servant explained that the ascetic had renounced worldly comfort to seek an answer to human suffering and the fear of death. These sights overcame Siddhartha, and the next day he departed his kingdom, abandoning his wife and son, to lead an ascetic life in search of a way to relieve the suffering of humanity.

Siddhartha strictly adhered to the ascetic path for years, yet the knowledge he sought eluded him. Sorrowfully, he sat by a river with his now five followers and stared at the flowing water. A young girl offered him a bowl of rice to eat; the prince ate the bowl of rice and bathed. At that moment, he realized corporal austerity was not the road to enlightenment: he discovered what he called the 'The Middle Way' – a life of balance in all things. Cleansed and refreshed, Siddhartha sat under a Bodhi tree and vowed to meditate until a god or some wise man revealed the truths he sought. He sat for several days meditating and purifying his mind. During his time in the wilderness under the Bodhi tree, Mara, a great devil, attempted multiple times to distract Siddhartha to abandon his quest; Siddhartha remained firm in his resolve, touching the ground, asking the Earth to bear witness to the revealed truth. Finally, a picture of the universe formed in his mind, and he knew he had solved the mystery: follow the *Middle Way* in all situations, consciously choosing to maintain balance through detachment from material circumstances and compassion for the inevitable suffering of human life. He became known as the Buddha or 'he who is awake.'

Why did I not choose to follow Buddhism? Although my exposure to Christianity was brief, I felt a more profound yearning for Jesus and the way of the Cross. Buddhism is a private practice with very little outward interaction with the priests; in coming to know myself, I realized that I did not possess the faculties to manage my life independently. Indeed I learned in Christianity that *my Creator did not intend for me to do so.* I needed the outward signs of God's grace to get through the days. I deduced that a more structured faith would assist me in growing in grace. The Catholic sacraments became that palpable, discernable vehicle to free me from my painful maelstrom and renew my mind. Jesus established His 'framework' – Holy Mother Church - to gather His flock and lead us along the path of righteousness. Jesus forgave me, washed me of my sins, and did not consign me to the punishment I deserved. His yoke *was* easy, His burden light. Jesus and the Church saved me and continue to save me every day.

I pray for my Buddhist brothers and sisters as they follow their journey, for it is a path of compassion, and that, along the Noble Path, should they hear the words of Jesus calling to them, may they recognize the summation of their heart's longing, 'lay down their nets and follow Him' - whether they hear Him in this earthly life or the next.

A DANCE WITH VISHNU

Hindus revere a formless, limitless, all-inclusive, and eternal god, all-powerful and universal, referred to as Brahman. It is Truth and Reality. Their scriptures, the Vedas, are the revelations of saints and sages throughout the ages. For the Hindu, the Vedas are as limitless as Truth is limitless, not entirely knowable yet constantly revealing itself. The very purpose of earthly life is to achieve 'dharma': right conduct, righteousness, moral law, and duty, endeavoring to always do the right thing to the best of one's abilities. Hindus believe that the individual soul (the *atman*) is neither created nor destroyed; it is eternal. The actions of each soul as it inhabits a body create consequences; each soul must carry these consequences to a subsequent life in a different body. This process of the movement of the atman to a new body is *transmigration. Karma* is the total of each soul's actions and the consequences of those actions; it is the summation of these consequences that determines the next body the *atman* inhabits.

As the soul continues to migrate from life to life, it has three paths it may choose to follow:

- The path of duty
- The path of knowledge
- The path of unconditional surrender to God

The ultimate goal: the soul's release from the unrelenting purification of transmigration, is *Moksha*. In Moksha, the soul recognizes its true nature, unites with Truth or Brahman, and is released from its earthly shackles.

Within the sacred writings of the Vedas is written the tale of the Bridge of Chahbot. The bridge starts on the edge of a precipice and stretches over a deep crevasse known as Chahbot. Despite the promise of unification with Brahman at the end of the journey, many souls, too afraid of falling off the bridge, choose to remain at the starting point on the ledge, trapped by the karma of their choices to repeat the same mistakes over and over and never move forward. Most souls heed the compulsion to be unified with God and start the journey. The bridge begins as a steadfast creation, firm under the foot, comprehensive, and safe. As the soul travels the bridge – transmigrating from one life to another – the atman gains knowledge and is inspired to continue. The further the soul travels, the greater the height and the narrower the way becomes, for with great knowledge comes great temptation. (I think the poet William Blake had this in mind when he wrote his famous poem, *Proverbs of Hell*: "The road of excess leads to the palace of wisdom"). Unfortunately, many climbers succumb to these temptations, lose their balance and fall to Chahbot. As I mentioned, the soul, the atman, cannot be destroyed. Those who fall into the pit must climb their way out. Many become discouraged, living eons in the darkness, wasting away at the bottom of Chahbot, prolonging their suffering and postponing their inevitable rigorous ascension.

As with Buddhism, the light of compassion towards one another was my first impression: I have observed that when Hindus witness another troubled human being burdened by the despair of selfish choices, they are called to compassion for *they recognize themselves in the sufferer, for we all travel on the bridge.*

The Hindu faith and Indian culture retain a special place in my heart. The concept of karma – accountability for our wrong choices and sin - seemed logical; however, as with Buddhism, reliving this earthly existence over and over did not. I imagined that if I believed in transmigration, I would have to repeat adolescence, mean girls, pimples, puberty, my 20s, arthritis, fad diets, cellulite, poison ivy, learning golf all over again, and waiting hours in the heat of a Tampa summer for the AC repairman to arrive. Seriously, this earthly life, however short or long, seems far too tricky a trial for God to require us to repeat.

The Hindu premise that our souls resided with God before our birth into human bodies did resonate with me, as it did when I first encountered the notion within Judaism; I discovered that these concepts were adhered to by first-century Pharisees and by the Catholic early church father, Origen. The most straightforward explanation I have come across that does not conflict with the *Catechism of the Catholic Church* is an article written by Father Gregory Wassen, *On First Principles, On pre-existence*, and published in 2016 in his blog, https://fathergregory.wordpress.com. He explains, 'A doctrine of pre-existence as such is not contrary to an orthodox and catholic view. In Origen's writings, he posits such questions as does the soul preexist? In his opinion, yes, in the sense that the soul is given from the hand of God and united to the body God created for it. No, in the sense that disembodiment is not the soul's natural condition, nor is there any form of reincarnation, nor is there any idea that the body is in prison into which the soul has fallen due to sin. Souls and bodies go together. They are *naturally* united by God's creational intent.'

Fr. Gregory's compelling and thoughtful analysis made sense to me; adherence to a pantheon of gods who each held sway over many aspects of earthly life did not. The gods seemed too inherently flawed in their human-like responses to circumstances.

This exploration into the concept of pre-existence resulted in an accidental curiosity about the Catholic church. In perusing church doctrine, the church never attempted to curtail my inquiries – indeed, the *Catechism of the Catholic Church* became a font of knowledge I utilized over and over. On the contrary, the Catholic church welcomed my quest, providing in-depth analysis and answers as opposed to what I perceived as a more simplified approach to faith in other Christian denominations. These investigations enhanced my view of God and His Son, Jesus.

In their excellent book, *Rome Sweet Home,* Scott and Kimberly Hahn speak about their mutual conversion to Catholicism. Both accounts were highly individual and compelling; however, in chapter five, Scott relates the story of buying out a collection of books left by the estate of a deceased priest and theologian, that it was within the process of reading and studying this acquired library which enlivened his new-found faith, sending him on the path to Catholic conversion. Finally, there was a Roman Catholic I could relate to; how delightful it was for me to realize that there are many, many Catholics who read, study, and participate in meaningful dialogue on church teaching.

I shall always be grateful to those Hindu brothers who instructed me, prayed with me, and enlivened my heart and soul with their teaching. They helped me find my true path. I pray for all my Hindu brothers as they climb the Bridge of Chahbot: may they see the Son of God waiting patiently for their arrival to welcome them home.

MOSES

Of all the religions I explored, one of the most compelling was the Jewish faith. The Jewish nation, recognized in Holy Scripture as pre-eminent among all countries, received the original covenant of God and retained its position as His chosen people. In his excellent book, *The Gifts of the Jews*, Thomas Cahill notes that our modern culture – and I refer to all of Western civilization – does not think a thought or read a book; indeed, our very day-to-day lives are influenced and governed by a culture inspired by God and assimilated and developed by the Jewish people. Although many philosophies contributed to the Judeo-Christian ethos, those of us who live in the West - Europe, the Americas, and Scandinavia, to name a few - are who we are because of the Jews.

The Jews believe that, after receiving the tablets on Mt. Sinai, Moses also recorded the oral tradition and beliefs of the Jewish faith, the oral traditions later coded and recorded in the Mishnah. The original five books attributed to Moses are known as the Torah (we Christians are most familiar with the Greek translation, the Pentateuch). Despite fighting for and claiming their ancient homeland, the Jews were overrun many times: by the Babylonians, the Persians, the Assyrians, and finally the Romans, and still further by successive foreign rulers after 400 AD. To create some structure for their community and to retain their spiritual practices and beliefs, the rabbis, scattered by their enemies across the known world, utilized the roads established by Alexander and then expanded and enhanced by the Romans to provide letters and commentaries to their people, helping them to apply Moses' laws not only to theological questions but to everyday problems. These communications of instruction and guidance provided a welcome cohesion for their culture no matter the outward circumstances and, especially during the time of the Romans, when most learned Jewish men were heavily influenced by and conversant in Greek as well as their native Hebrew and Aramaic. Recorded in Hebrew and Greek, messengers and tradespeople carried the scrolls along the fast, efficient Roman highways to their brethren living in outlying areas. At the dawn of the new millennium, rabbis gathered these commentaries and edited and combined them into cohesive volumes that evolved into what became the Talmud – a 28-volume magnum opus filled not only with theological opinion but efficient, practical solutions to everything from how to settle community disputes and household dilemmas, to parables illustrating points of Torah, guides for married life, and recipes, including how to prepare a chicken. The Talmud is a seemingly endless knowledge repository essential to the Jewish people.

In studying the Jewish faith, I began to feel closer to Jesus. Visiting Israel and walking His pathway, standing in Peter's house, sitting in the center of the synagogue where Jesus first announced Himself, I felt His presence – His *Jewish* presence - in a way I hadn't previously. My study of the Torah and the Talmud has been essential to my final baptism as a catholic: by reading Torah, I came to understand some of what Jesus meant by fulfilling the covenant with God, tracing the thread of events throughout the Old Testament that foretold His arrival and the monumental impact of His life, teaching, healing, passion, and death.

Judaism was the first tradition to teach monotheism. As history evolved and God revealed Himself to His people, the Jews recognized God as the One unknowable, universal, image-less Being. The design and creation of all living things is an act of love. Therefore, for life to flourish abundantly, life's sustenance necessitates the correct behavior and justice from the human beings God created to steward the planet and its inhabitants. Made in His Image from the same love with which He created human beings, God endowed them with sovereignty over his earthly creation.

In reading the Torah, especially after studying parts of the New Testament, I felt a wonderful sense of history, but a story half told. So much emphasis is on cause and effect: do this, and you will be happy; do that, and punishment ensues. The chronological story of the Jews records their often wayward behavior and lack of obedience, and for their faithlessness, they suffered the Lord's judgment. Yet it is the Lord's continual efforts throughout salvation history to communicate with his people and to warn them to correct their ways. Considering the trials and tribulations the Jewish nation has endured from its earliest beginnings over the millennia, 5,000 years of slaughter and mayhem, to the Holocaust of the 20th century, Judaism has remained a beacon of faith and contributed more to civilization than we may even recognize. Our salvation story began with the Jews; we owe them a debt.

The cohesion of the community, the sense of history, and the eternal are all present in the Temple. I was entranced. The services are beautiful; the faith of the people is palpable. I recall the shivers in my arms as the Cantor recited their greatest prayer, the *Shema*:

> *Hear, Israel, The Lord is our God, the Lord is One.*
> *Blessed be the Name of His glorious kingdom forever and ever,*
> *And you shall love the Lord your God with all your heart and*
> *with all your soul and with all your might,*
> *And these words I command you today shall be in your heart.*
> [Deuteronomy 6:4-9 NKJV]

The knowledge of the Torah and Talmud became another lantern on my way to my Christian formation.

I found yet again that compassion was the watchword; indeed, one of the year's holiest days, Yom Kippur, the Day of Atonement, if properly adhered to, provides the faithful Jew forgiveness and redemption of the past year's sins. Notations made on their behalf in *The Book of Life* are wiped clean. With the advent of Rosh Hashanah, the New Year, they start again with a refreshed spirit and strengthened resolve to avoid sinful behavior.

The story I paraphrase below comes from the Talmud and, for me, illustrates the generosity of spirit, forgiveness, and mercy of Christ, a son of David:

> At the insistence of his youngest son, a king divided his kingdom into two halves between the oldest and the youngest. The oldest remained with his father to learn to rule justly and to be of service; the youngest sold his share of the property and traveled to a distant city in a foreign land where he spent the entire amount on wine, women, and song. Not hearing from him for a year, his father was concerned and sent a messenger to bring him back home. The messenger found the son homeless and trying to earn money for wine. The messenger asked the son to return to his father's house; the son declined – he said he preferred

his life as it was. The following year the father sent the messenger again to bring his son home; the messenger found the boy starving and destitute, sick and near death, eating whatever fell in the street. The messenger begged the boy to return to the father's house; the son declined, saying, 'I have gone too far; I have brought shame to my father's house. Tell him I am dead, for I cannot return as I am.' The messenger returned to the king, reporting on his youngest son's condition, shame, and refusal to return home. The father returned the messenger to the boy, telling him, 'Come as far as you can, and I will come the rest of the way.'

In light of the Old Testament definition of justice and its emphasis on an eye for an eye, I am reminded of Jesus and his gift of redemption and salvation, His *redefining* of the very meaning of the word 'justice,' and the effect Jesus' life has had on the entire world, including the Jews. Jesus led me to forgiveness, the treasure at the end of the rainbow, where the road of justice and the path of love intersect.

I remember the first time I sat in a Catholic church; I found a seat in the back pew. Mass was already underway, and the priest was reciting a prayer. A sense of calm washed over me; I immediately recognized I was in the right place.

Jesus did not approach me in celebration: no flags flying, no drums drumming; simple, unassuming, quiet, and respectful. Instead, he posed a question, 'Follow me?' The next moment I heard bells ringing three times and saw the priest raise the Eucharist above his head with such reverence and profound humility I found I could not look away. My heart seemed to beat out of my chest; my eyes filled with tears. I distinctly remember feeling a familiar presence, one I had felt when I cried out silently amid those terrible midnight encounters with my father: that same warm presence, at once comforting and inviting, and in my heart, I seemed to hear a gentle voice say, 'Can we start now?'

I was home, but different from the home that I had previously imagined. I had wandered in the wilderness for forty years as I was turning 40 in less than a year– and had finally found where I was supposed to be.

Now I carry my baptism certificate wherever I go – a reminder of the precious gift of admission to the Kingdom of God. Jesus washed away the hurt of my childhood and the pain of my sins. My Redeemer has revealed the true path to salvation: through Him, with Him, and in Him, in the unity of the Holy Spirit. In his book, *Just As I Am, Billy Graham remarked* that 'suffering is part of the human condition, and it comes to us all. The key is how we react to it, either turning away from God in anger and bitterness or growing closer to Him in trust and confidence.'

The insight I gained from my years of study opened my eyes to the possibility of beauty and wisdom all around me. I learned to recognize God in the most unexpected places. And in that recognition, I experienced His Mercy and Grace, which, over time, gave me the courage to forgive both of my parents. Finally, I understood the pain both had sustained in their families of origin. Acknowledging their pain was the beginning of my forgiveness of my parents, a huge step that required all the courage I could muster, as it was one of the hardest Jesus had asked of me. But in obedience to Him, He set me free.

CS Lewis, a theologian I greatly admire, noted, "I suggest to you that it is because God loves us that He gives us the gift of suffering. Pain is God's megaphone to rouse a deaf world. You see, we are like blocks of stone out of which the sculptor carves the forms of man. The blows of His chisel, which hurt us so much, are what make us perfect."

We are called to this life, born of woman, and carrying the burden of sin from Adam. Here, in this earthly existence, this valley of tears, the Lord's presence in Heaven obscured from our vision, He allows us to be tempted so that we may know His Mercy. In this life, we are called each day to the path of righteousness to perfect ourselves and return to Him as his faithful children.

I give thanks for the abuse, neglect, abandonment, love, and tenderness I received in my life and all of my experiences. They were profound teachers, and I learned compassion and forgiveness from them.

I also give thanks for having been born with the minor affliction of blindness in my left eye; Jesus taught me to see differently, to recognize the mighty works He completes in every moment, and to trust in Him whom I could not physically see.

I am grateful for each step along the long path that led me to the

Savior. I learned to find common ground with those unlike me: to seek unity where there is estrangement and, to my surprise, to be charmed by the unexpected. The knowledge I gained during those years is invaluable, and I am thankful daily for my new life in Christ.

Humans will continue to suffer as long as human sin abides. Therefore, until He returns for us, I choose to serve Jesus, obey Him, and pray that He continues to help me to be worthy to serve His church.

Chapter 9
GIFTS OF THE LOST SHEEP

'...If he has committed any sins, he will be forgiven. Therefore, confess your sins to one another, that you may be healed.'

JAMES 5:15-16 NRSV

'If I had cherished iniquity in my heart, the Lord would not have listened.'

PSALM 66:18 NRSV

IN MY LIFE, GOD HAS blessed me with miracles. Whether He has touched me with His healing power, or someone I know, I am amazed by each gift. And I am not unique. I have fixed my mind, eyesight, and perception upon the miracles of God and the beauty He creates at every moment. It is entirely a product born of my choice to surrender my self-determination and my life to Jesus, a voluntary act of my free will, strengthened by the charity and grace of God.

In the Book of Matthew, Jesus assures a Roman centurion who approached him in Capernaum, requesting that He heal his ailing servant. Jesus responded affirmatively, "Go; let it be done for you according to your faith." [Matt 5:12 NASB] granted the centurion's request out of the soldier's recognition of who Jesus was and His power to heal. The Roman centurion further states, 'Lord, I am not worthy to have you enter under my roof; only say the word and my servant will be healed. For, I too, am a person subject to authority, with soldiers subject to me. I say….”Do this, and he does it.’ The centurion’s submission to the authority of God has been noted many times, but it is the humility of this pagan soldier I find so poignant. A recognized military leader with power over 600 soldiers, as well as a Roman citizen, referring to himself as unworthy of entertaining an itinerant Jewish holy man is remarkable.

A significant component of faith is *loving* God. If we choose to love the Lord, we enter into communion with Him, returning to Him that he pours out to us every moment. His grace, charity, and forgiveness are our rightful inheritance. Our failure is in not asking for it. In describing God’s love for us, perhaps it is Shakespeare who said it best, “…I wish but for the thing I have. My bounty is as boundless as the sea. My love as deep. The more I give to thee, the more I have, for both are infinite”. [Shakespeare, The Tragedy of Romeo and Juliet, Act 2, Scene 2, Lines 133 - 136]. Historically, we have attributed this expression to erotic love; however, it is the willingness of the lover to give the love, recognizing his compensation is in his expression of that love. Every parent knows this: I loved my daughter as she grew in my belly, my heart bursting when I first glimpsed her face, although she did not understand who I was. As she grew older, my forgiveness of her childish transgressions was swift and consistent. She just had to ask, although I often forgave her before she did.

In faith, as in loving God and admiring the beauty he creates, the more I choose to employ my faith, love, and worship of Him for Himself, and to recognize the beauty He creates, the more confidence I receive, the more love I feel and the more beauty I experience.

This new-found hope in my heart and a deeper appreciation for God’s creation are the gifts of my conscious choice to speak the truth about myself and relinquish my sins to Jesus. Appreciating the Lord’s magnificence and engaging my faith is far easier without the limiting hindrances of shame for past sin, resentment, worry, and hurt. These distractions cloud my perceptions and confuse my mind. The beauty is always there, but in my distracted self-involvement, I pass right by it. The Lord knocks at my door, but I am self-centered to hear Him.

Although James assures us most emphatically that Jesus will bless us if we take the difficult first step of confessing our sins, no human on

Earth probably finds this easy. I know I didn't–and still don't. Although I regularly avail myself of the sacrament of reconciliation or confession, it never fails that my mind goes blank as soon as I sit down to read off my list of transgressions. I cannot recall the simple prayer to begin the sacrament, and I even get a little dizzy. So I've learned to bring my handy *Catholic Book of Prayers;* I open my trusty book and read the opening prayer from its helpful contents. This small ritual centers and prepares me to relate my sins to the priest.

For those unfamiliar with this sacrament, confession of your transgressions to a priest, whom Catholics recognize as acting *in persona Christi*, and under the authority of Jesus, through the apostles. The admission of sins and the request for absolution places my errors at the foot of the Cross. Yet, as the priest thoughtfully considers what I have imparted, there is a slight pause before I hear that I am absolved. Even though I am nervous and embarrassed, that fractional pause reminds me it is not the priest who is forgiving me. As Mother Teresa of Calcutta said, he is 'God's pencil.' [Professor Mary Poplin, see Bibliography] Christ works through the faithful priest to forgive me; Christ Himself is absolving me, the only one who can.

This theological point was paramount during my search for God. Although the Lord already knows what sins I have committed, the exercise of confession–of speaking to His representative, for a Catholic, an ordained priest, or a fellow Christian if you are not Catholic - is a humbling, cleansing, and necessary exercise on the path to forgiveness. While not all religious affiliations recognize or require another person or priest to be present, necessitating only a frank admission of sin in private prayer, I found that adhering to the practice of my acknowledgment of sin in prayer did not elicit my longed-for renewal or bring me closer to Christ. I am afraid I am too prideful; it was easy to spend my prayer time negotiating with Jesus, 'Well, I know you are already aware of _____, so I don't need to repeat it....' As a long-time participant in a 12-Step program, I recognize the power of Step Four, a searching and fearless moral inventory of ourselves. To experience real change, I need to admit to another person the errors in my thinking and actions.

Another reason I ultimately embraced the Catholic sacraments was the emphasis on surrendering to a power greater than me. I wanted healing for my warped thinking, to make better choices, and become closer to Jesus. And I knew, from years of trying, that I was incapable of either truly believing Jesus had healed me or changing my behavior on my own. Even after therapy, as I became more and more comfortable with my past, there remained deep inside a little river of misery, always keeping proper restoration and peace just a little out of reach. *Someone far more powerful and intelligent than me had to heal this.*

Whatever your beliefs, I realize how daunting it is to consider this step, especially for a returning Catholic. However, you know what is at stake if you are a fellow Catholic. A priest confessor, glimpsing my palpable embarrassment through the screen, once told me that Jesus waits in anticipation for our confession so that He may demonstrate His profound mercy and forgive us. Knowing that Our Redeemer eagerly anticipates my confession so that He may forgive me helped ease my awkwardness. Pope Francis echoed this teaching in his *Sunday Address, Regina Caeli, [see Bibliography/End Notes] May 22, 2022: 'God never ever tires of forgiving us! ...the problem is that we ourselves tire, we do not ask, we grow weary of asking for forgiveness. He never tires of forgiving, but at times we get tired of asking for forgiveness.'*

For as long as I can remember, my closest friends, family members, and my husband have all commented on how closed off I can be; my most intimate friend Marsha, who has known me about 50 years, said recently, 'I may have been your closest friend, but there are so many barriers you keep up, only revealing parts of yourself to me.' Although I may have felt protected, my secretiveness kept me separate from others and God. Yet, I can attest to His power of forgiveness and the peace that comes from reconciling with Him. Marsha elaborated, 'In these later years, I see such a change in you: you are open, glowing with the love of Christ!' we all tend to be reluctant to share ourselves, to hide: Satan lives in the shadows, the light is of Christ. Adam and Eve hid from God in the garden because they had sinned and lied about it; the shame kept them skulking in the bushes, afraid to reveal themselves after their transgression.

Like many people, the years of my early adult life are punctuated with mistakes I regretted: unmarried sex, smoking pot twice, drinking with my friends, and driving home-who-knows-how from a bar a couple of times. Picking yet another fight with my ex-husband. Each time I would ask myself, *Why did I do that?* I was the quiet, steady type, the good girl my mother could count on, ever-ready to assist in dodgy situations and choose sensible solutions. These missteps were not habitual behaviors, but my actions before my baptism spoke to my hurt, loneliness, and lack of spiritual guidance. In floundering and flailing about, I would confide in my mother, who would look at me askance at my embarrassment and remind me of her sage advice on human foible: *the word sin is a Greek archery term; it means you 'missed the mark.' So what? Let it go. Walk it off.* I tried to follow her advice; however, my conscience would not let me. My recovery helped me recognize that I was not bad, yet I kept concluding that wrong behavior was terrible and proper behavior was correct. I could see that my sinful behavior had a corrosive, erosive effect on my self-esteem. My parents may have been cruel and abusive; however, the shame I felt over these mistakes spoke to my interior belief that I *should* feel ashamed as I was essentially wrong–a defective part of the Universe–and I deserved to feel that way.

As I mentioned, I began therapy in my early adulthood – group and individual sessions - to help me examine the abuse I suffered as a child and learn new and better coping methods. Even after the years spent exploring these painful episodes, the most challenging aspects for me to grasp were where it didn't initially appear as though I was at fault, yet these same incidences kept repeating in my life. It took much uncovering for me to recognize my participation in these situations. I unconsciously selected men who behaved towards me like one or both of my parents. I also intentionally or unintentionally provoked the other person. If it was intentional, I manipulated or goaded in some other way, picking a useless fight to get back at a real or imagined slight. Finally, I would dramatically wave my arms, appalled, lay the blame on the other party involved for dramatic effect, and, with a flourish, slam the door behind me. Much of the wrongdoing belonged squarely at my feet. Although I did fume at how infuriating the other person was, I secretly congratulated myself that I had had the last word.

Though I might get a bit carried away, this behavior was a clear, conscious choice and, thankfully, correctable. The more significant, deeper problem lay in the fertile ground of my unconscious: I felt unloved, unwanted, useless, and slow-witted. In these discordant situations, the provocation was unintentional: I consistently selected the exact man who could be relied upon to slap me, hit me, take my money, lie to me, rape me, or leave me homeless. Lying on my girlfriend's couch yet again, counting my measly funds and hoping to rent another apartment, I knew I *deserved* this.

Perpetuating this belief, I selected a husband who was possibly more wounded than I was. Raised by an alcoholic father and a mother who desperately tried to hold her family together, my ex-husband suffered from the disease of alcohol and drug addiction. My ex-husband's alcoholism was not as apparent before we married; it was after our garden ceremony. After that, however, his struggles became obvious. My ex-husband did not battle his demons; he tried to escape them. He was drinking with his buddies until the wee hours of the morning, blatantly unfaithful and neglectful.

However wrong his behavior was, I could be relied upon to respond in an unhelpful way. Throwing a pizza at his head and a log from the fireplace at his precious Porsche were not responses recommended in the Al-Anon Big Book. No one was better than me at righteous anger! I can still recall one of my therapy sessions where I had spent the first half an hour emotionally flailing about, condemning my alcoholic husband for cheating on me yet again. My patient counselor pointed out that 'co-dependents and co-alcoholics are often the most difficult people to work with; they can be self-involved.' *Self-involved? Me? He was the one who got drunk again! He slept with her!* I left that session with serious doubts about this therapist; she had got it all wrong again.

The next day, at an Al-Anon meeting, I continued my refrain of blame and condemnation, repeating the incident for yet another group of ready and willing listeners. The newer members nodded in recognition, agreeing with me; however, the members who had worked the program longer, like my sponsor, counseled me to 'turn your husband over to a Higher Power and concern yourself with *your* behavior and program.' *Say what? Are you kidding?* I still wanted to throw something at my husband (oops, wait a minute; I already did that).

I have since learned that Jesus does not look into our hearts and attribute guilt in the way my human perception would have expected. When I accuse a brother or sister of sin and then report a litany of their crimes to Jesus, invariably, divine attention seems to boomerang back to *me*. I recalled Jesus' instruction, concise and perfect, 'You hypocrite! First, remove the beam out of your own eye, and then you can see clearly to remove the speck out of your brother's eye.' [Matthew 7:5, WEB]. Ok, but sleeping with her is not a *speck*! Over time, in prayer, the Holy Spirit helped me to see that, although my husband committed a terrible sin (more than once!), I had also contributed to the breakdown of our marriage. I remember chatting with my ex-husband years later about the pizza-thrown-at-his-head incident, snarling at him:

'Why did you like her so much?'

'She had a great butt.'

'I had a great butt! All those girls were alike, always praising you to the skies! So, of course, you chose them!'

He smiled at me and replied, 'Yeah, that had a lot to do with it.'

I looked at him, astonished. Then we laughed.

It was a lesson I always remembered.

When I imagine life after death, purgatory, and all that may or may not come with the after-death experience, I often wonder: what does Jesus say to criminals when they die? How does He forgive Hitler? Idi Amin? My father? In my relationship with my father, I was a child and blameless about my abuse. Yet I ultimately recognized, and had to confess, the sin *I* committed out of my resentment and hurt, the damage this hurt and anger did to *me and others*, and how *I had kept myself* from a closer relationship with God. Many of the sins I committed originate from these resentful, hurt feelings. I wanted to belong to a man that would love me, but I would invariably choose men with traits similar to my father: angry, harsh, critical, and wanting me only for sex.

After their release from Egypt, the ancient Jews wandered in the wilderness for forty years, lost and confused. Having arrived at almost 40 years old in my own life, relationship to relationship, still uttering the same refrain, 'My parents were terrible, my life ruined, and it's all their fault.' Yet it was after I turned to the Scriptures, specifically in reading about some problems Moses faced leading a fractious group of confused, recalcitrant people out of slavery across a vast desert to the long-promised land, that I recognized a pattern of the events. Despite direct communication from the Lord, the Israelites often fell prey to discouragement, returning to their pagan gods for comfort. Humans lose heart so quickly, becoming intractable and disobedient, as with the ancient Jews. It never occurred to them that their lack of faith and rebelliousness kept them lost for over a generation.

Despite his loyalty and obedience to God, Moses, too, fell prey to discouragement and ebbing faith in Meribah. In his momentary despondency, this great leader lost the privilege of living out his life with those who stayed faithful; Moses was never allowed to step foot upon the Promised Land. Although he had led them out of the vast desert of Zin, God relegated the great prophet to a distant hilltop to view the longed-for arrival at the promised land from afar and then to die on that hillside alone. The lesson is clear: *the circumstances may seem unfair, even hopeless; however, faithlessness speaks to disobedience. And disobedience distances us from the very source of our well-being, safety, and love, leaving us alone in our self-imposed exile.* Through much of the 40 years, Moses demonstrated remarkable faithfulness: when the people cried out, he did not lose heart. Time and again, Moses obediently turned to the Lord for help. However, by the time of his arrival, Moses had allowed the constant clamor of the people to wear him down. Upon the arrival of this tattered and fractious group in Meribah, Moses' faith was dissolving. The Lord called him out, *proclaiming to Moses and Aaron, 'Because you did not believe in me, to uphold me as holy in the eyes of the people of Israel, therefore you shall not bring this assembly into the land that I have given them.'* [Numbers 20:12 ESV]

Scripture is clear: a faithless response to overwhelming or unfair circumstances may cause an irreparable loss. *'But whoever has doubts is condemned if he eats, because the eating is not from faith. For whatever does not proceed from faith is sin.' [Romans 14:23ESVUK].* After forty years of trials and tests, Moses lost his faith in the Lord for one fleeting moment and never placed a sandal on the Promised Land. For me, the healing process included recognizing that my destructive anger camouflaged deep hurt and woundedness, fueling my decisions to sin (and make no mistake, it is a *decision* when we sin). Sin is a turning away from God. Even if caught in a vortex of guilt, confusion, and regret, turning away from God results in a more profound fall into the abyss of self-condemnation.

My advice is to make an appointment with your parish priest or pastor. Fall on your knees, open your heart, and humbly admit your transgressions. Then, with a 'humble and contrite heart,' accept the offered grace. And I purposefully include the instruction to *accept the grace offered*: you may discover, as I did, that the act of *receiving* the healing grace of God is, itself, a *submission* to God. I liken this to the arrival at an ER, where you must sign a waiver to *submit* to the treatment offered and recommended. Accepting Divine Grace is admitting your powerlessness to correct your life on your own, a genuine surrender of your will to the power of the only One that can truly heal you. It was Napoleon at Waterloo, Lee at Appomattox: a complete capitulation.

Do not rob yourself and those around you of a healed heart and a peaceful mind. Why do I include your loved ones? There is a palpable difference in living with and relating to a person who has faced their demons, stated their truth unequivocally, and received the grace and restoration of God: they are kinder, more patient, and far more accepting and understanding of other people. A new trend in bumper stickers and tea shirts encourages us to 'Be Kind.' It is a lovely sentiment; however, if your spirit is heavy with unacknowledged anger, guilt, resentment, and regret, the already faulty human capacity for the generosity required to be kind, limited by our fallen nature, may be temporarily non-existent. *We cannot give what we don't have.*

Open your heart to Jesus, tell Him of your sorrows, your mistakes, and how you choose at this moment to repent of those errors and to sin no more. Ask Him to forgive you. Pope Francis explained that forgiveness of our sins is not something we can give ourselves; forgiveness comes from Jesus: 'Forgiveness is not the fruit of our own efforts but a gift. It is a gift of the Holy Spirit who fills us with the wellspring of mercy and of grace that flows unceasingly from the open heart of the crucified and Risen Christ.' [*General Audience, February 2014*]

To prepare for this sacrament, I encourage you to write it down, even if it's just a list of bullet points. Every moment you were less than you could have been. Whatever mistakes you may have committed – every ugly thought – write them down and take them to the Lord. Confess your sin to Him and prayerfully ask for His forgiveness. Then, for your own sake, include *every* sin, even *that one.* I will not sugarcoat this step: I cried a few times out of shame and self-pity, but slowly I embraced the gift of grace this act of trust and honesty offered me.

I decided that a trial run before I confessed to the priest would help me feel less nervous, so I read the entire list to my best friend, the ever-trusty Marsha, whom I have known since I was 17. Already aware of most of my peccadillos, Marsha was embracing and encouraging, and I felt better having related these facts out loud to someone else first. A few days later, when I officially confessed, I accepted full responsibility for each sinful act and asked for the Lord's forgiveness. Still, as I was not a baptized Catholic yet, absolution would come with my immersion in the baptismal font.

Although complete immersion was not standard previously, many new converts opt for total immersion as I did. As they lowered my face and body into the cleansing water, I *felt* the Lord's forgiveness: His love's warmth swept over me and filled my heart. Photographs of that day still astonish me; my face looked lit from within. I stepped out of that baptismal font renewed by the Holy Spirit. God had cleansed my soul from the bottomless font of Jesus' Mercy. One of my friends asked me if God would accept my baptism without the step of confession. Absolutely. As an adult convert, my confessor and I believed this step was integral to my particular preparation for baptism. However, as affirmed by Legionary of Christ Father Edward McNamara, professor of liturgy at the Regina Apostolorum, "the sacrament of baptism is the door to the other sacraments, and no sacrament can be validly received beforehand. Second, one of the primary effects of baptism is the total forgiveness and wiping out of all sins committed before the reception of the sacrament. For these reasons, confession before baptism is impossible and unnecessary.' Father McNamara further emphasizes the importance of confession, stating that for the previously baptized, "The case is different for a person who has been already baptized in the Protestant denomination and is to be received into the Catholic Church. In this case, confession is recommended before formal reception and confirmation.'

Jesus takes us only as far as our free will dictates. So I chose the only absolute freedom – the release from sin, guilt, shame, and anxiety: the freedom of His Love and forgiveness.

I have spoken many times of the power of the Sacraments as one of the chief reasons it attracted me to the Catholic Church. Jesus designated Peter and his fellow apostles to assume the keys to the Kingdom of Heaven (Matthew 16:19 ENSB, Matthew 18:18 NASB), including the power to forgive sin (John 20:23 ESV), a departure from the original covenant with Moses and unheard of in ancient Israel. Although the confession by a disciple of Christ originates from the early church, I learned later that, in this form, we trace the act of confessing to an ordained priest back to Saint Basil the Great in the 4th century. After its inclusion into Christian practice, this sacrament underwent further study, investigation, and discussion before finally being upheld by the Council of Trent in the 16th century. Throughout these centuries, the forms of confession, absolution, and penance evolved through many practices. From what I have read, we can thank the early Celtic church and monasteries established in Ireland for providing the basis of the currently accepted form of the sacrament of reconciliation. As introduced in 1973, the Rite of Penance is not limited to the Roman Catholic Church: this sacrament of mercy and redemption is a recognized and integral rite included in the Anglican, Lutheran, Methodist, Russian Orthodox, and Greek Orthodox churches, to name just a few. In the tradition of repentance for the Hindi religion, they included a warning in the *Holy Bhagavad Gita* against overzealous adherence! This notion of forgiveness and penance is a concept that has resonated through the centuries in many cultures. In Jesus and His church, one experiences the fullness of God's Mercy.

As mentioned, I became familiar with performing a confession when I joined a 12 Step recovery support group. The 4th through 7th steps outline the systematic process for the admission and confession of errors and the request to a Higher Power to remove these 'shortcomings.' Although I joined Incest Survivors Anonymous with a few minor revisions, our organization closely adhered to Alcoholics Anonymous, the worldwide support organization recognized as one of the most effective treatment programs for alcohol and drug dependence. Created by founder Bill W. the twelve steps provide a progressive system of steps based upon the need to accept powerlessness over changing your life. Proper adherence to the steps, in their prescribed order, includes a full accounting of, and honest contrition for, the errors committed.

Participation in reconciliation and receiving the Lord's absolution was essential *to my baptismal* experience. By honestly relating as much as I could recall, I surrendered yet again to Jesus and His Saving Grace. This act of contrition is an actual act of faith, for not only does it require a surrender of all that you are and all that you have done, but the contrite must also possess a sincere belief in Jesus and His power to redeem you, or at least be willing to believe that He can. I approached my first confession, my walk of fire, knowing that I had tried everything to overcome the abuse I suffered and all the mistakes I made, and only an all-powerful God could release me from this pain and forgive me for my sins. I looked another human being in the face, told the truth about myself, and gave it to God, believing that He was the only one with the authority to forgive and heal me.

In further preparation for my baptismal sacrament, I read chapter VII The Grace of Baptism in the *Catechism of the Catholic Church*, 1262. Newly re-published within months of my upcoming rite by St. Pope John Paul II, the introductory statement of fundamental truths in the Catholic Church. Stated definitively, "By Baptism, *all sins* are forgiven, original sin and all personal sins, as well as all punishment for sin. In those who have been reborn, nothing remains in those who have been reborn that would impede their entry into the Kingdom of God, neither Adam's sin, nor personal sin, nor the consequences of sin, the gravest of which is separation from God." (CCC, No. 1262)

As I write this, I can remember that day clearly: I stepped into that water, strong hands grasped me securely, and I felt myself descend. Before that day, I was apprehensive about being lowered backward. Now, in complete trust and submission, my eyes closed, my body went *down*; the water slowly enveloped me, and I remained under for a moment. There was no noise, no tremble. Although the water passed over me, I was not alone at the bottom. In his *Letter to the Romans,* St. Paul speaks of, '…we who were baptized into Christ Jesus were baptized into His death…We were indeed buried with Him through baptism into death, so that, just as Christ was raised from the dead by the glory of the Father, we too might live in the newness of life.' (*Letter to the Romans,* 6:3b-4, NAB) In a split second, I felt a death within my body - discarding the unwanted, a shedding of an outer and inner layer no longer required. A second later, Jesus' anointed minister tightened his grasp and lifted me to the surface, raising me to the light and my new life in Him. *He lifted me; I did not lift myself.* Jesus stayed with me in the depths and carried me upward into His embrace. For a moment, I was stunned, silent, blinking about me at all the people gathered around the font. And at that moment flashed the recognition that He and I had been in the depths together before: in that bottom bunk bed, in the dark, with my father. Jesus had been there with me; He never left my side. In moments of heightened fear and injury, pain and humiliation, there had been a presence; *someone had been there with me*. At some of the worst minutes, a pale light would appear, and I would follow with my eyes and in my mind. The light led me away from what was happening – I felt emotionally detached, a reprieve for a few blessed moments– and then I would return to the scene calmer, quieter. This presence appeared several times, and I learned to trust it – *to turn toward the light*.

So I did, at the bottom of the baptismal font: I turned towards the light, feeling the solid and safe arms reach for me, grasp me, and pull me to safety and communion. Jesus washed me clean right then, and I was reborn in the Holy Spirit. My inner Shield Maiden, that fierce warrior that had protected me for so long, willingly dropped her sword and laid down her shield. My contemplative side, the most genuine part of me, was finally free to express herself. In His forgiveness, I discarded the shame of my childhood and the guilt of my adult errors.

Several acquaintances would ask Michelangelo how he created the David and the Pieta; he replied, 'The sculpture is already complete within the marble block before I start my work. It is already there. I have to chisel away the extra material.' So, Jesus, the Master Creator, did for me: He removed the excess anxiety, fear, shame, and regret expertly disguised as outspoken, righteous anger and revealed a heart softened by His mercy. He peeled away the extraneous, the unnecessary, to reveal his original creation: who I truly am and who He created me to be.

Surprisingly, I have become one of those friends acquaintances feel they can confide in. At first, I attributed these skills I learned as a psychiatric nurse; now I know it was, and is, my willingness to be honest with Jesus and myself, which has fostered a new intimacy with others. As they relate their history to me, I understand and empathize with those terrible feelings of shame and guilt. St. Thomas Aquinas speaks of a 'sorrow, of the supernatural order.' He distinguishes the human fear of the punishment – the bed we make that we each must lie in – and what St. Thomas refers to as 'attrition' and the transcending regret of sin for sin's sake. As defined by St. Thomas, a motive of filial fear causes true repentance. I found this to be true in my own life: after my baptism, in contemplating God's response to my sinful choices, my motivation for correction shifted from appeasing

God or, more often, bargaining with God (*Please fix this, and I'll never do it again*) to a conscious distaste for the behavior itself, simply because my conduct was intrinsically wrong.

For approximately two years after my baptism, having failed to retain my spotless, baptismal soul, I had imagined Jesus disappointed in me if I committed even the tiniest mistake. Over time and many studies of the Gospels and the Catechism, I began to realize that if it were true that I had disheartened Jesus, He would be disappointed *every day*, for every day, no matter how hard I tried, I transgressed. It was then that I came to understand the true nature of the Trinity: supreme, omnipotent, and *eternal*. My errors did not change Him; they changed *me*. He does not possess a fallen nature; I do.

My human transgressions are still frequent yet venial as I foster a closer relationship with Jesus, and not because I fear He may be disappointed in me: I find myself less and less attracted to those behaviors. Sitting in my pity pot crying over spilled milk, mumbling to whoever will listen how badly I blew it is a purgatory for me and misery for the poor listener. Still, admitting, *Dear Lord, I blew it the same way again*, is truly lamentable. Suffering with the same remorse over and over became just too painful; I found it best to return to the confessional and regain that 'peace which passes all understanding' [Philippians 4:6 ESV] or, better yet, avoid this mistake altogether. The light has become too attractive as Jesus fills my heart with hope.

Over the years, I have read and re-read the passage, *'By Baptism, all sins are forgiven, original sin and all personal sins, as well as all punishment for sin. In those who have been reborn, nothing remains that would impede their entry into the Kingdom of God..'* from the *Catechism* many times, primarily to convince me that the Lord has truly forgiven. I was, and am, accountable for my sins. Now it is time to accept the Lord's forgiveness and to be who He created me to be. It was proper that I should suffer as I did. But I cannot allow it to block my energies or heed my call to His Purpose: prolonged grief and victim sorrow enlarge the actual suffering and can be self-indulgent. My baptism was 40 years ago. It is time for my heart to open more fully to Jesus and to step out of this chrysalis of pain. There is so much to be done! Jesus must increase, and my old burdened self must decrease.

About two years ago, I started volunteering in prison ministry. Over two years ago, I volunteered to facilitate several programs servicing a 2,000-inmate prison for men, approximately an hour from my home. The gentlemen selected to participate in these programs do not have the luxury of scheduling their own time or the privacy to read and study; they must work as they can. And they work hard. Despite their confinement's inherent difficulties, each is diligent and committed. Although not all are comfortable writing, they read the assigned passages and discuss them with their friends in class.

The most striking thing about them is their integrity, purpose, compassion, and honesty. Several of them will never leave a locked facility. Each of them has experienced depression, hopelessness, and despair. Yet within the confines of a less-than-hospitable environment, they are carving out a life of purpose.

Unfailingly honest about the circumstances that brought them to the prison, I shared my story with them. In that group room, we are united as sinners, possessing a shared equity in acting out of a fallen nature and creating a reality in our lives less than what our Lord intended when He created us.

In these classes, the Lord has blessed me and all of us with a group of men committed to a life with faith at the center, reflecting honesty, sincerity, and purpose. As the Lord heals my heart, I feel compelled to reach out to the less fortunate in my community. The Lord's lost sheep. Those lost sheep showed me compassion, kindness, understanding, and empathy. When I speak of regret, they know exactly how I feel.

As a young man, my father was incarcerated several times before joining the merchant Marines to avoid another jail sentence. How I wish someone would have reached out to him, shared the love of God with him, and helped him recover the man the Lord created him to be. I pray he knows I have forgiven him and that Jesus has redeemed him.

I pray.

Chapter 10

THE BIRTH OF THE
SHIELD MAIDEN

IN MY QUEST TO FIND God, addressed in later chapters, I briefly studied the Viking runes: their mystical origin, how the ancient Scandinavians used them, and the accepted interpretation of their symbols. My study, cursory at best, led me to the Norse legends of the shield maidens and their supposed origin, the Valkyries.

One of the most famous of these warrior women was Brynhildr Buoladottir of the Volsunga saga. The story relates that Brynhildr expected to be wedded to her chosen mate, a warrior named Sigurd, but as the story unfolds, a friend tricks Brynhildr into marrying her brother instead.

Delving into the Volsunga saga, it becomes apparent that Brynhildr's overriding focus was to live honorably and forthrightly and follow the Viking codes of conduct. However, her burning hatred toward those who had tricked and betrayed her undermined her life's purpose. The story ends in a series of battles in which Brynhildr obtains revenge upon her treacherous husband. In a storm of self-righteous furor, she kills her husband and his son from a previous marriage. In the heat of the battle, when her compatriots question her actions, this brave and noble fighter attempts to justify the murder of her husband and stepson. Although the Vikings were known as fierce warriors, then as now, murder is murder: the Norse gods allow this brave shield maiden to die in battle as punishment for her actions. Despite the betrayal of those she had loved and trusted, Brynhildr felt justified in executing her offenders, failing to see that in her hurt and anger, she, too, had sinned in exacting such a loss of life.

My father's business ventures, bolstered by my mother's monthly paychecks, had flourished so that, just before my 15th birthday, my parents bought their first house together—a three-bedroom ranch-style home on an inordinately large lot. All of us, except Mama, were thrilled it had an oversized rectangular pool. My sister and I had our rooms, and I could enjoy evenings of solitude and peace, alone in my own space, reading or listening to records. My parents, preoccupied with decorating their new home, had declared a *détente*. We seemed to have turned a corner. It would not last long.

Daddy's participation in the home decreased markedly within six months of our relocation. Daddy's absence coincided with a renewal of my mother's prolonged, pouting silence. She would start another knitting project, refusing to acknowledge Daddy's presence whenever he came home. Several months later, I would learn of the underlying cause of this marked deterioration in my parents already fractured relationship: three agencies of law enforcement -the IRS, the FBI, and the local police department - launched a joint investigation of Daddy's business in suspicion of racketeering, fraud, and tax evasion.

Our suppers became a silent No Man's Land between enemy camps. Mama refuses to speak to Daddy or even look at him throughout the meal. Daddy never raised his eyes from his plate. I would eat quickly and retreat to my room. Mama's sulking silence and Daddy's petulant grumbling had become reliable harbingers signaling the ongoing disintegration of my parent's relationship and heralding the resumption of our family's violent drama.

The kitchen became the family Alamo. My mind still carries reels from the memories of our brand of family commotion, at once scary and humiliating. Both Mama and Daddy participated in the violence. Our home became a three-ring circus: on one side of the house, we have Mama, furious with Daddy for his criminal activity and aggravated with herself for forgetting to defrost supper, flinging frozen pork chops through the glass window of the back door, narrowly missing the back of Daddy's skull.

Now enraged with Mama for nearly breaking his skull, unable to find me hiding outside, Daddy raises his clenched hand at Mama, and she bursts into tears. In a split-second, Daddy pivots, landing a solid punch to KO the kitchen cabinet. At that point, I ran back into the house and hid, cowering under my bed, waiting for the screaming to stop. When the IRS sold our home two years later, the scars from our domestic tumult - great gashes in the walls tattooed parts of the house – belied my father's invention of our happy family.

My father's belt renewed its preeminence in our home. High school lost whatever small pleasure it had brought me up to that point, and my grades dropped, resulting in my failing geometry. Embarrassed by my welts and bruises, I retreated into opaque silence, detaching even further from my classmates, skipping classes here and there to hide in the library and read alone. I had no friends.

Mama's depression began to slowly strangle her remaining hope. When she got home at night, Mama would walk to her bedroom, change her clothes and lie down. Meals became catch-as-catch-can. My mother's suicide attempts occurred during this period and, as I realized later, consistently happened when I was home with her.

My mother tried to take her own life several times during this time. In each episode, I was the one home with her. She had always been deathly afraid of water – she couldn't swim a lick after nearly drowning at the beach as a small child. On this particular night, though, Mama arrived home from work, parked the car, put her purse down, and, not saying a word and still wearing her work clothes, ran past me through the house to the backyard and jumped into the deep end of the pool. I heard the splash and dove in after her. After bringing her to the surface, she fought me off, clamored out of the pool, and ran into the bathroom. I stumbled after her in time to see her flinging the medicine cabinet open, locating her sleeping pills, then emptying the bottle into her mouth. I grabbed her around the middle and squeezed, forcing her to cough up the drugs. She screamed at me, saying I was hurting her. When I let go, she fished a pair of scissors from the drawer and tried to stab herself in the heart. I managed to pin her against the wall, holding her there until she finally seemed to calm down. As I stepped aside, she started to cut her hair off but then attempted to slit her wrists. Holding her tightly again, I wrenched the scissors away from her grasp and led her, wet and trembling to her bed, where she sobbed for at least an hour. Today I know that suicide attempts are a desperate but misguided cry for help. It must have been so for Mama; somewhere in her sorrow, she knew I would never let her die.

The birth of the Shield Maiden changed my life. It was the summer before my senior year in high school, and a full year had passed since the last suicide attempt. The weather was hot and dry outside due to the seasonal Santa Ana winds. Standing in front of the kitchen sink, drinking a Coke from a glass bottle, I remember gazing into the front yard and noticing how the tree branches swayed in the afternoon breeze. I wasn't aware of the impending danger at first; Mama's scream across the house and my father's heavy footsteps stomping towards the kitchen—the familiar signals that my father's anger had erupted—warned me before he came through the kitchen doorway. I pivoted to face him. My father uttered something unintelligible and raised his closed fist toward me. At that moment, something inside me snapped – I just saw red. Still clenching it by the neck in my right hand, I slammed that glass Coke bottle against the porcelain divider in the middle of the sink. Then, holding the jagged edges of the remaining portion of that Coke bottle against my father's throat, my eyes staring straight into his, I growled, 'If you hit my mother or me, you are going down.' My father froze, his fist clenched and suspended above my head, the edges of my Coke bottle still poised close to his throat. He remained frozen for about a minute, staring into my eyes as I stared back at him. I did not waiver. I did not blink. After another minute, Daddy lowered his fist, turned slowly, and left the room. My father never struck my mother or me again. The Shield Maiden was born.

From then on, my anger burst into explosive fits, usually directed toward my mother and, later, my ex-husband. If I had a barometer to measure the wrath quotient of my fury, it would have varied depending upon the degree of disappointment or hurt I perceived in any circumstances. As a child, when faced with setbacks, hurt feelings, or scary situations, I would respond like a wounded bird, fold my wings, and stay still, silent, and afraid. Then, after her birth, the Shield Maiden would emerge in a nanosecond, bypass any feelings of fear and hurt, directly to the shield-up-spear-ready stance of a warrior. *It wasn't going to happen to me again.*

In the case of my most important relationships, the Valkyrie of my bottomless anger laid waste to all offenders. However, the warrior woman within me stoked the fires of my long-held resentment toward my parents, especially my father. I hated him! Long after I left home, the embers of hatred for both of my parents, which seemed dormant by my mid-20s, still burned hot within me.

It was almost ten years later before I began to realize that my proud and dependable self-reliance was hampering my ability to experience peace, joy, and happiness. Even after I married in my early 20s, serenity, peace, and genuine closeness to my new husband eluded me as I clung to my ardent independence. My self-reliance guided me through heartbreaking and often dangerous situations, bringing a massive dose of self-deception. Times that I felt I was ok, I was still in survival mode, not at peace. As with my heroine, Brynhildr, I failed to grasp my contribution to the marital estrangement within the first year of my marriage. I achieved marginal safety in my emotional life but not the depth of feeling I had often dreamed of. My true feelings remained bottled up, unable to find expression.

Through the healing processes of Catholic spiritual formation and active participation in the 12-step support group Incest Survivors Anonymous, I became aware of my feelings. I realized how destructive my behavior had become. I also realized that my self-reliance, vital to me as a child, had morphed into the veiled sin of false pride. This singular refusal to truly trust another person or to look deep within me kept me from the promised land of authentic human love and affection. Instead, I measured each encounter against an internal yardstick for potential damage, humiliation, and danger, expecting each friendship to end sourly. In those years, my life resembled the ball in a pinball machine: bouncing off one obstacle or disappointment only to slam into another. I was forever *reacting* and not *deciding*. It never occurred to me to ask for help. Instead, I concluded that life would not be peaceful; I mistook pride in my endurance for happiness. In my pain, I figured that men and women would always disappoint me and that I could only rely on myself.

Marital counseling led me to join a noisy, raucous, divorced women's group. In one session, we listened to a group member extol the benefits of throwing herself precipitously into a whirlwind romance after years of avoiding intimate relationships. As I listened to her amusing anecdotes about traveling with a new boyfriend, my jaw dropped when our therapist blithely commented, "You know, 180 degrees from sick is still sick."

The astuteness of that observation hit me like a ton of bricks. I remember musing, *look at my life - my best thinking got me here.* I could thank the Shield Maiden for guarding my daughter from sexual and physical abuse. In truth, her warrior-woman defense of me and my child had broken the chain of generations of incest, and I was grateful to her. Yet both character types: the shy, depressed child and the ferocious shield maiden, resulted in a lack of intimacy, trust, and joy in my life. Any intermittent, random insights into my behavior could be derailed by the hyper-vigilant Shield Maiden, who thought she was protecting me. My brave inner warrior helped me graduate from college, successfully circumventing the self-fulfilling belief derived from my parent's judgment that I was 'dense as a stone' and would never amount to anything. However, the Shield Maiden could do nothing about my inner denouncement of myself as the lonely, emotionally incapacitated daughter of abusive and neglectful parents who deserved the treatment she received. I had not healed the wounds of my abusive childhood: my Shield Maiden, the 180-degree opposite of the shy, frightened child I used to be, and who had protected me from further abuse by my parents and others, was a camouflage, a defense mechanism that deflected others, as well as myself, from the knowing the truth about me: I was still that hurt little girl. My memory had cemented the image of that shy little girl hiding under the bed with her doll in my brain. Inside my heart was a wounded five-year-old girl masking her fear of being hurt behind false confidence, still seeking love and approval from my mother, which would never come.

I had made significant progress after four years of therapy and support groups. I was no longer depressed; I had cultivated reliable, close friendships and supported my daughter and me with a job I was proud of. However, as with my childhood home life, relative peace and calm did not last.

Meeting a fellow participant at a spiritual retreat and telling myself I was ready, I entered another volatile relationship. The former self-sabotaging behavior – the outward expression of my belief in my mother's pronouncement that I was 'dense as a stone' – emerged again, starting with me quitting a fantastic job to relocate my daughter and me to my new boyfriend's home. Unfortunately, unbeknownst to me, he had continued his other relationships. A year of confusion and unhappiness culminated in his disappearance one evening and, despite multiple phone calls, not returning home until the following morning.

This clear breach of trust in our relationship triggered my Shield Maiden, who had been lying dormant for a few years. The Shield Maiden's fury confronted my boyfriend as he entered the door. An all-day argument, interrupted only by his nursing a hangover and my need to feed my daughter and his boys. The day came to a tumultuous climax of violence in front of my daughter and his children as he grabbed me around the neck, choked me, and forced me to the ground. He then began to kick me, then dragged me by the hair to the front of the house. After he threw me into a wall, I managed to grab my cell phone, but just as I dialed 911, he knocked it out of my hand. Fortunately, the call had connected, and the agent remained on the line long enough to track our home and send a squad car. The police officers charged into our home; the first officer located me under a table, and the second officer coolly confronted my angry partner. By now, he had calmed down. Within minutes they had secured my partner in another room away from the kids and me as the three of us discussed the next steps. I was reluctant to press charges; however, the cuts on my face and bruises on my arms, back, and chest belied my claim that 'everything was ok now.' The police officers handcuffed my assailant and led him to the squad car. I joined the children; as we all peered out the windows, that man stared back at me with intense hatred and anger. I was terrified.

The next day as I was reflecting upon this incident with my therapist, I realized that this incident was just one of a series of similar episodes over the last 12 months; none of them came close to the degree of this one. However, a pattern of steady amplification of tension, followed by shouted epithets and thrown objects, had increased month by month. It was clear to me that the trajectory of my life seemed to have been spiraling downward. Unhealed wounds drove my thinking, incapacitating my rational thought and ability to make healthy choices. It was clear that the many years of therapy had not deterred me from being attracted to men whose behavior echoed my family of origin and my own my internal belief: I am unworthy, unlovable, and undeserving. An off-hand comment by a staff psychiatrist with whom I had an on-again-off-again relationship years ago flooded me:

'You are beautiful, brilliant, and broken. It is a miracle you came out as well as you did.' Perhaps I was hopeless.

It was painfully apparent that my divorce years before and now the violent end of this new relationship was both so explosive that even with my usual ability to sublimate what I preferred not to think about, there was no denying the underlying truth: I had reached a point where I knew the kind of change I needed was beyond my capability to produce. Yet, unbeknownst to me, I had taken the first step towards recovery in that moment of clarity when I knew I was powerless to fix my unmanageable life.

As I look back upon my marriage, many in our circle of family and friends were secretly relieved we had separated. Family, friends, and neighbors felt the effects of this latest destructive relationship deeper than I had anticipated. Neighbors approached me, supermarket cashiers inquired, acquaintances and friends of friends offered their condolences, and even a prayer group from a church I had attended only twice sent a note to let me know they were praying for our family. This community involvement - the general awareness of my circumstances – was a new and confusing phenomenon. I am an adult survivor of incest: keeping secrets was all I knew. The arrest of my boyfriend in broad daylight alerted the neighbors to the danger in our home. There was nowhere left to hide. I was outed. The dissent into the family tragedy was complete: I lived with another alcoholic, abusive philanderer who echoed my ex-husband's and my father's behavior. In moving in with him, I had endangered myself, my child, and his children. I coped with the situation using the same classic tools of crying, begging, screaming, threatening, and locking him out of the house. Nothing worked. I had failed.

My boyfriend never returned to our home. After his release from jail the next day, he sent his parents to retrieve his clothes and belongings. We met once at the therapist's office, where I promptly reverted to my trusty Shield Maiden stance, hurling accusations, insults, epithets, and threats. He looked at the therapist with a "Now, do you get it?" smirk, and she looked back at him in recognition of his point. The therapist managed to elicit a promise from me to stay silent as she knew that my husband had some things to "get off his chest." He proceeded to list the numerous extramarital affairs he had conducted since before our relationship began, confessed to $80,000 of debt I was unaware of, and to spend our entire mutual savings. In the final summation of his *mea culpa*, he ended our relationship to pursue another woman. It was over. As I walked back to my car, the realization that, having turned away from the sheer power and intelligence that had been healing me and relying upon my instincts, warped by abuse and tragedy, I had not only lost my savings; I had endangered my daughter, been beaten, and abandoned.

After our allotted hour had concluded and my now ex-boyfriend left, I stayed for another session. In shock from my boyfriend's admissions, I was finally able to utter a *mea culpa* of my own: my Shield Maiden—that part of me I treasured and relied upon—may have saved me from dangerous situations several times, yet it too was as flawed as my warped instincts, responding to hurt with furious anger and contributed to almost ruining my life. How could I possibly think it was a good idea for all five-foot-two-inches-and-one-hundred-eight-pounds of me to stand up to a six-foot-one-inch-two-hundred-pound drunk and enraged man and further ignite his anger by getting in his face and screaming at him? How is this a successful life strategy? And why did I stay in this dysfunction?

I had spent my adult life up to this point striving to avoid my mother's mistakes and the pain of being the helpless victim I was as a child. I had relied upon my flawed thinking that at least my Shield Maiden stuck up for me and 'set the record straight.' However, hearing from my next-door neighbor, who made a point of regaling me with all the tidbits she overheard, her recollection almost entirely of my voice hurling insults, left me profoundly embarrassed and ashamed of my behavior. Of course, I never blamed myself for his abusive behavior; hitting another person is wrong, period. Even so, it was painfully evident that in my decades of effort to take the polar-opposite approach from my mother's coping skills - silence and disdainful avoidance - during my childhood, it was painfully apparent that my behavior still managed to replicate the horrifying home of that childhood. My long-time therapist was right: 180 degrees from sick is still sick.

Yet after I left and began to face the scary prospects of raising a daughter alone again, I found myself repeating my pattern and turning to my trusty Shield Maiden. She assured me that I could cope with anything:

that I didn't need to be hemmed in by the ending of a bad marriage, a terrible subsequent relationship, and expired notions of weddings or committed love. I was now free to enjoy short-lived relationships that did not require the depth of honesty or feelings implied with a commitment. What did it matter if I was living paycheck to paycheck? My Shield Maiden encouraged me that a new outfit, a new man, or an expensive meal in a new restaurant would cheer me up. She encouraged me to find new friends unconnected to my past, who did not raise concerns over what I was doing or who with. She reminded me that I was the victim and it was my turn to enjoy life.

Despite this new mode of thinking, I kept faithfully attending therapy and support groups. Slowly I began to understand that although these behaviors helped me temporarily escape my unhappiness, they also prevented me from looking at the deeper wounds I refused to recognize.

In my heart, I believed that the experiences with my father carried a kind of stigma that others unconsciously perceived. Under the anger, I discovered a more profound humiliation at the core of my woundedness. I learned that living with some level of chagrin ever present in my life was where I was comfortable, so I unconsciously chose men who helped me to re-enact these painful scenarios leaving me where it was familiar: feeling unloved and humiliated. I could always find a man to criticize, slap, or abandon me for someone else. The sexual abuse at my father's hands had occurred at such a young age that the reality of shame was more comfortable than being loved. As a student nurse, I witnessed children separated by child protective services from their abusive parents at the county hospital on several occasions. One drug-addicted mother had burned her child's arm with cigarettes, yet when the sheriffs gently pulled them apart, the child screamed for the mother who had just burned her. That was me; I was that child. No matter the suffering, abandonment was worse. That was my truth.

My trusty therapist, to whom I shall always be grateful, felt there was still something else I hadn't uncovered. She was right. Lying just below the profound shame I felt from my experiences with Daddy was the ground level of my emotional and spiritual pain: my mother's abandonment, rejection, and lack of protection for me as a child. There were many instances when we faced Daddy's terrifying rage; Mama did not protect me; she ran to her bedroom and locked the door, leaving me to face my father alone. She could hear me screaming and glass breaking, but she refused to leave the safety of her bedroom. During Daddy's midnight wanderings to my room, Mama would awaken but did not intervene. Mama hid the evidence, tossed the notes from the school nurse in the trash, ignored the bruises, and sent me to the bathtub with bloody legs. She hushed up the doctor. Mama knew and allowed the abuse to continue.

My wise and insightful therapist, who had stuck with me this far, once talked about family dynamics, identifying the roles each person in the family unit would play and their influence over the family. Almost all of us in the audience were adult children of alcoholics; when she asked for a show of hands as to how many would identify the noisy, often violent, alcoholic parent as the most emotionally damaging to us as children, almost all of us raised our hands. Finally, she nodded and replied, 'You always want to watch out for the quiet parent; they can hurt you the most.' So it was for me. Mama's unwillingness to protect her child was perhaps her greatest failure.

The moment of realization that my angry behavior, a by-product of my fear, and born the moment I held that Coke bottle in defiance of my father's threats, had contributed to the failure of my marriage, often hurt my daughter's feelings, and cost me several friendships, was a profound awakening to the truth. I realized that I could sometimes be difficult with my colleagues at work. I had a chip on my shoulder containing the pain and hurt I endured as a child in my heart. *I had assumed aspects of the angry, belittling criticism that my parents had used on me. No, I was not abusive, but in my continued harboring of resentment towards them, I had assumed characteristics of the very persons who had hurt me the most and who I dreaded above all else to become. Yes, they had abused me; but I had been unkind to myself and others who had hurt me, berating and cursing them. For example, when I caught my ex-husband cheating, I threw a pizza at his head in front of my baby daughter.*

In the support groups and 12-step organizations I was affiliated with – Al-Anon, Incest Survivors, and Co-Dependents Anonymous – I met other men and women who were wrestling with these same challenges: yes, they had suffered at the hands of alcoholic spouses, abusive parents, and friends who took advantage of them, yet were finally forced to come to terms with the dysfunction in their behavior.

But, unfortunately, hurt people tend to hurt people.

After this tumultuous relationship ended, and as I progressed in therapy, I spent years alone, not dating, spending time with my daughter, working, attending meetings, exercising, and frequenting bookstores. This extended period of cocoon time, when I sometimes spent all my free time away from my daughter alone, allowed me to integrate what I was learning in a group. I worked the 12-Step program faithfully but kept getting stuck on step number two: *I came to believe that a power greater than me could restore me to sanity.* I had accepted that there was a 'higher power' and that he could restore me to sanity. Yet I felt outside of his grace, his sphere—an outlander.

I am grateful to God for a three-in-the-morning crisis of spirit two years later when it was too late to call friends nearby and too early to call loved ones out of state. That fateful night was just me, a sleeping child, and the profound weight of my mistakes. Physically depleted from recent surgery, I sat on the floor in tears of despair, realizing that I had contributed to the break up of my marriage; I remembered how it felt to be left by him, broke and alone with a little girl, not knowing how I was going to pay my rent. I began to berate myself for all the mistakes I had made, with still no idea as to how I could fix my life. I looked around my studio apartment and felt a terrible fear that maybe nothing had changed; perhaps all my hard work over the years would fall by the wayside as I would probably end up with another abusive man.

I hit my bottom: on medical disability from work, broke *again*, and fearful of the future, I could look no further down; for me, there was no further down to go. I fell to my knees, reached up, and with tears streaming, surrendered to God. In my mind, I could see Jesus on the Cross, alone and abandoned. In my tears, I asked Him how He could want me like this. I kept telling him I was not worthy of His love; I'd ruined everything. Then, deep within me, I heard Him say, *come to me now, daughter, just as you are.*

So, I did. I gave Him my hurt, humiliation, and all the mistakes in my life that, at that moment, I could recall. I told Him how alone I felt and admitted that I knew of Him but had assumed that He liked everyone else but me, or He wouldn't have allowed me to be abused, neglected, and unloved. I confessed my anger at Him for what I saw as His abandonment. I told Him my anger felt bottomless and then admitted that I could not heal this anger or stop the hurt and that I had no idea how to solve the problems in my life by myself.

What I was sure of was that my anger had contributed to my divorce and this last breakup. The life I had planned for my daughter and myself would not happen. Looking back upon my marriage, I also know that my ex-husband did not marry me to be unfaithful or become an alcoholic; he married me because he loved me. Together in our woundedness, we had wounded one another very deeply. I recognized that I did not drive my ex-husband or ex-partner to drink or into another woman's arms but contributed to our estrangement. I then became clear about what I had to do.

As I lay on the floor, still teary, I pictured in my mind leading my Shield Maiden to the Cross and laying her down at the foot of it. I thanked her for all the service she had performed for me; for the many times she came to my rescue when I needed help or was afraid. I thanked her for being the one person I knew I could count on until now and that she taught me to face whatever scared me and have courage. Before I said goodbye, I explained to her that how she helped me no longer served me and, in some cases, created havoc. What scared me now was that I might be stuck forever as an angry 16-year-old adolescent. Clasping her hand, I thanked her again from the bottom of my heart and left her with Jesus, asking Him to forgive us both. I fell asleep on the floor, at peace.

As the days passed, a strange certainty emerged: peace. Finally, admitting I was powerless to fix the mess that had become my life and that this profound recognition of my brokenness had been a fundamental first step towards a new life. I felt humbled in asking for and accepting the help, support, and love I required. My desperate prayers were answered, and the cavalry arrived. I no longer had the strength to fight. Over time a new humility, something kinder, quieter, and without a trace of shame or embarrassment, ensued within me in recognition of the new life the Lord offered: a meekness, not a weakness, that stripped away the Shield Maiden's false pride and allowed God's healing love to move through me. In the newness of faith, as I felt the love of the Lord wash over me, I realized I had to open those raw places, the deep hurt pocket in my heart, and allow the light of Jesus to pierce me and move through me. I remember a school nurse dressing my bleeding legs once: she was very kind and warned me that the ointment she used would sting me, but I would heal better if she used it. It did sting, but I healed perfectly with no scar. The light of Christ moved through me, cleansing and illuminating and, for a second, stung. *The more I surrendered my will and spirit, the less it stung.*

In those first few weeks, I observed myself revert to the quieter, more contemplative person I was before the Coke bottle incident. I would feel transitory alarm, sensing my new-found vulnerability, and begin to feel afraid. Not well versed in forms of prayer at that time, when I experienced a disappointment or disagreement, I would find a place to be alone and, in my mind, say, *Jesus, do you see what just happened? This is it! Right there. I am feeling afraid; I don't like feeling scared. But I want to avoid making the same mistake. Please help me do it differently. Please show me what I need to know.* And He would. I could feel a calm assurance overtake me; my breathing would slow down, and I could return to what I was doing in a minute or so.

In his Letter to the Romans, Paul admonishes his followers, 'Do not conform to the pattern of this world but be transformed by the renewing of your mind.' [Romans 12:1 NIV] Self-help books had terrific advice and techniques to employ for helping oneself. But that was my problem: my pain and woundedness ran deep, *and I could not help myself.* The self-help books left me feeling more discouraged, and I would say to myself: *I tried that. I should be better by now. What is wrong with me? I am unfixable.* I needed someone much stronger, wiser, capable, and intelligent to fix it. Admitting the truth to Jesus that I was lonely, afraid, and worried was essential to help me remain humble and open to instruction and correction. Jesus helped me to replace my negative thoughts with life-affirming faith and change my fearful, marred perception to crystal-clear knowingness. *The more I trusted Him, the quicker the relief came.*

The Lord extends Himself in love, for it is the essence of who He is. To accept His love and help when I had tried so hard for so long on my own was to feel the warmth of His acceptance begin to soften my heart—a heart hardened by false pride and disappointment. The 'softening' part was intensely moving. Each time I trusted Him, I could feel another section of the stiff outer shell I had built over my heart crumble, leaving my soft heart with more room for His love. It still does.

In these times of what I began to call 'my joyful pain' – these feelings of my stiff heartbreaking – I started to recognize what was at the core of my isolation. It was not a fear of rejection as I had supposed; it was the wrenching dread, fraught with anxiety, the same message Mama had drilled into me for as long as I could remember – that I *was* unworthy, unlovable, and slow-witted as a stone – might be true. My deepest fear was that my devoted friends, educated therapists, sponsors in recovery, and medical doctors had, out of kindness, lied to me: my deepest fear was that everything that had happened to me – all the abuse and neglect - was because I *deserved it*. My parents had been right all along.

Loving God and accepting Jesus as my Savior brought me to my eternal salvation and the hope of Heaven after I die, but the Savior also graced me with a genuine peace right here, *right now*. In loving Jesus and allowing Him to love me, I learned to love myself and my brothers and sisters. Only Jesus offered me a genuine opportunity to start over, to do it differently: to break the cycle of family dysfunction that had dominated my thinking and dictated many of my choices. My parents may have been abusive towards me; in the game of childhood, my hand wasn't the best, but I had doubled down on that pain by abusing myself as an adult with my choices. In surrendering to God and accepting the dominion of a loving Father, I was submitting to leadership that was infinitely wiser and more charitable than me. As my thinking started to change, so did my observations: I began to recognize Christ within my family, my friends, my acquaintances, and myself.

My surrender to God has given me a greater acceptance of my limitations and true vocation: to love Him and my brothers and sisters. I recognized that it was never the Lord's intention that I live my life as an angry Lone Ranger; He created me to love Him, worship Him, and turn to Him for all of my needs. Asking for, and accepting, help when I needed it was a step of profound humility that set me free of the past. The Lord extended Himself and His Love to me and gave me the grace He knew I needed to receive it.

Fast forward to the present, and I occasionally relapse into Shield Maiden Mode, especially when the stakes are very high, or something serious happens to my family. *For the rest of my earthly life, I must continue to surrender the Shield Maiden to the Lord, laying her down at the foot of the Cross, thanking her for trying to help me, forgiving her for her insensitivity, and reminding her I am not an abused, beaten, neglected five-year-old little girl anymore. I whisper to my beloved Shield Maiden: you may sleep now; rest in the arms of the Blessed Mother who loves all of her daughters and who advocates for each of us.*

In the Virgin Mary, I found the mother who will never abandon me, will never betray me, and leads me back every time to Her Son, who also loves me and died to save my soul. As I return to Cross, I sheepishly approach His presence, embarrassed by my latest mistake and fearful of taking another step toward Him and failing. In my mind, I can see myself lying at the foot of the Cross, feeling broken and unworthy yet again, and I hear the echo of ancient scripture whisper in my heart, 'Talitha koum. Little girl, get up and walk.'

Chapter 11

NOT TODAY, SATAN

$\mathcal{M}$Y WALK WITH THE LORD has not been easy; there were times at first when I questioned my Catholic baptism. Being a Christian of any denomination is not choosing the simple path: C. S. Lewis stated, "I didn't go to religion to make me happy. I always knew a bottle of Port would do that. If you want a religion to make you feel really comfortable, I certainly don't recommend Christianity."

Why would this be? Is discouragement inevitable for the new Christian still immersed in the joy of a recent baptism? Those of us who have some years of faith can attest to the difficulty in walking the path of light.

My entire preparation-for-baptism process was two years of prodigious study, learning to pray and meditate, and living as an observant Catholic. Delving into scripture with my new tool, the *Catechism of the Catholic Church,* was very interesting; however, I must confess, a little part of me felt busted. I couldn't help comparing my old life and familiar choices to what I now knew I should have done in the past, hoped to do in the future, and was not doing in the present. So I peer up at my new crucifix on the wall sheepishly, like Jesus caught me red-handed.

After twenty-eight years as a full-fledged Catholic in good standing, I assumed that I had reached a deeper level of comprehension in my faith life: I regularly participated in daily Mass, daily devotions, and daily Examen. I also learned from my years in 12 Step programs that were more effective when volunteering to make coffee and set up meetings every week, ensuring my participation each week and reading recovery-minded books. So when the opportunity to facilitate weekly Mass for inmates at a prison near me presented itself, I volunteered. After a year of faithful service, the diocesan ministry group offered additional participation in a restorative justice program, and I readily accepted. When the chaplain allowed me to facilitate a new class at the beginning of my second year, I jumped at it.

Throughout my Catholic life, I have regularly volunteered for different projects: membership in a diocesan deanery for restorative justice, facilitating Catholic women's programs, and as a board member of the local chapter of a global women's ministry. The prison opportunity would call upon skills I learned as a psychiatric nurse in a large California state facility. Working in the huge admitting unit, we regularly treated physical and psychiatric emergencies, including patients strung out on Angel Dust experiencing AFIB, drug addicts attacked and robbed, and hallucinating people with schizophrenia who assaulted someone in their family. In addition, the sheriffs would bring in their 5150s - persons they observed acting to harm themselves or another person - and we would keep them in our locked unit for 72 hours of evaluation. Our psychiatric medical staff was exceptionally skilled; I assisted the doctor that evaluated Charles Manson. In addition, state prisons, specifically Folsom, would regularly transfer inmates that exhibited psychotic issues for evaluation.

My psychiatric nursing experience was varied and extensive, especially in emergency, adult services, drug addiction, and incarcerated patients. After ten years on the floor, I moved up to administration in the private sector, working in marketing and program delivery services. This experience was exciting as the teams I worked on devised integrated programs utilizing the various disciplines in a coordinated effort to assist the patients in stabilizing, recovering, learning new skills in coping, and returning to their lives.

The new class I would facilitate utilized established and well-regarded video and workbook materials to provide the inmates with a well-rounded historical and theological study of creation through the first 50 years of the New Testament. Comprehensive, with significant reading, and produced by a Catholic university, the bishop of my diocese agreed to underwrite the expense of the videos and workbooks if the prison chaplain approved the material. The chaplain insisted that the class, while utilizing Catholic materials, must be more ecumenically focused. As a convert familiar with the protestant Christian perspective, as well as Quoran, Torah, and the Vedas, I was excited at the prospect of the discussions we would have in the class and readily accepted his terms.

After ten months, our core group in the classroom were committed men working very hard towards a closer relationship with the Lord as they understood Him. The class agreed to divide each chapter into small pieces. At this point, the men had completed almost half of the program modules. New administrators had arrived the previous year and supported the programs offered in the chapel, including mine. Several times a few of the highest administrators stopped by to sit in on our classes, and the men welcomed their interest.

The warden and several of the administrative team invited us to breakfast in the chapel to thank us for our hard work. As I walked into the breakfast, the prison chaplain stood up and declared that I was his 'blonde for a day .' Parodying my nickname of Kat, he called me his 'kitty...look how I make her purr' and started stroking my hair. I froze. I just sat there. I could feel my face become hot with embarrassment. Finally, one of my colleagues from the diocese entered the breakfast, and I moved to sit next to him. Still, this person persisted, placing his face next to mine until the warden, who had just seated at our table, stopped him. I stood up and left to attend my class, humiliated. After all these years of prayer, baptism, sacraments, therapy, volunteering, and happy marriage, when someone is sexually inappropriate with me, I still freeze, failing to protest or protect myself. I made it through my class before feeling physically sick, barely making it to the restroom before vomiting, then crying, so disappointed in myself.

Retelling this incident to my fellow volunteer, she asked me why I didn't drag him to the hallway and read him the riot act. I started crying again and expressed my shame at freezing vs. fighting, telling her it felt like I was five years old again, freezing and staying very still. She replied knowingly,' Of course it did. That is what you were taught.' I burst into tears, feeling more ashamed: But I wailed; I should be better by now.

Over the next few days, as I worked with my husband to compose a letter confronting this person, I kept hearing that accusatory voice, Why are you still acting this way? What is wrong with you? You are unfixable. I fell into a shame spiral that lasted two days. Finally, I sent the email to the prison chaplain, who readily apologized, and I considered the issue closed. The man in question had apologized; I had resolved the problem. But my shame spiral continued spinning. What do people think of me? Are my wounds evident to everyone? Will I never heal?

Several days later, as I prayed in preparation for my monthly spiritual direction appointment, Jesus appeared to me in my mind, His body lit from within, wearing a bright gold tunic with a colorful collar, His face serene. A light shined from behind, illuminating His entire body, and I noticed that despite his beautiful garments and glorified body, His wounds were visible. He said, 'Daughter, I never appear without my wounds. Your wounds are beautiful. They are perfecting you. Do not try to hide them.' and then vanished.

My eyes still fill with tears at the memory of this moment. Jesus healed His lost child of the shame of my old wounds and the lasting effects I still suffer. I share these visible wounds with my brothers and sisters, for we are all wounded in our ways. This earthly life is a purgation, a time of perfecting to ready us for our return to the One Who Loves Us Most. For years, I have worked hard to suppress these wounded areas, not to pressure my husband and our marriage, fearing that he would leave if he saw how wounded I was. Jesus' appearance at once spoke of His love and acceptance of who I am, how I am still hurting over the past, and His recognition of my suffering. He also wanted me to know how close He is to me and that He is accessible anytime.

So now I will stop trying to suppress these feelings; I will acknowledge all parts of myself and pray for the grace to offer them to the Lord. Then, with the help of the Holy Spirit, I will be more honest about how I feel and trust my husband to accept and love me. I give thanks for my new freedom in Christ: freedom from stifling my deep pain, freedom from the temptation for self-criticism, freedom to authentically me, and freedom from being 'Stone,' frozen, and afraid.

The next time I hear that voice say, 'Aren't you better by now, Stupe?' I'll reply out loud, 'Not today, Satan.

BIBLIOGRAPHY

06 06 2018 UNTIL PRESENT

- Transliteration, Tanakh, sefaria.org.
- Nelson, Thomas (author); Holy Bible: New King James Version. Thomas Nelson, 2018
- Holy Bible New Living Translation, Zondervan, 2022
- New Catholic Bible, Catholic Book Publishing, 2021
- New International Bible, Zondervan, 2017
- Saint Augustine of Hippo, *The Enchiridion on Faith, Hope and* Love, 420 AD Aeterna Press, 2014
- NRSV Bible Translation Committee (Author), Bruce M. Metger (Translator); *The New Revised Standard Version Bible with Apocrypha* (Oxford University Press, 2006)
- NASB New American Standard Version
- WEB World English Bible
- ESV English Standard Version
- ESVUK English Standard Version Anglicized
- His Holiness, Pope Francis, *Regina Caeli*, Sunday Address, Saint Peter's Square, The Vatican, 22 May 2022.
- Holy Bhagavad Gita, chapter 17:28
- His Holiness Pope Francis, *General Audience*, February 2014
- Shakespeare, William, Wilson, John Dover(Editor), *The Tragedy of Romeo and Juliet, The Cambridge Dover Wilson Edition* (originally published/performed January 29, 1595; this edited version: Cambridge Library Collection 1921) Act 2, Scene 2, Lines 133-136

- Poplin, Professor Mary, Finding Calcutta; *What Mother Teresa Taught Me About Meaningful Work and Service.* (Downers Grove, Illinois, InterVarsity Press, 2008)
- Donald Senior, John J. Collins, Editors, *The Catholic Study Bible, The New American Bible* (New York: Oxford University Press, 1990, 2006)
- R.P. Thomas Pegues, O.P., translated from the French and Done in English by Aelred Whitcare, O.P., *Catechism of the 'Summa Theologica' of Saint Thomas Aquinas, For the Use of the Faithful',* New York, Benziger Brothers, Printers to the Holy Apostolic See, 1922
- Tr F. Max Müller, in *Buddhist Parables*, by E. W. Burlinghame, 1869; reprinted in *Sacred Books of the East*, volume X, Clarendon/Oxford, 1881; reprinted in *Buddhism*, by Clarence Hamilton; reprinted separately by Watkins, 2006; reprinted 2008 by Red and Black Publishers, St Petersburg, Florida, the first English translation (a Latin translation by V. Fausböll had appeared in 1855)
- Robert Moynihan, Ph.D., *Let God's Light Shine Forth, The Spiritual Vision of Pop e Benedict XVI* (New York: Crown Publishing Group, 2007)
- *Child Maltreatment 2006. Washington DC: US Department of Health and Human Services Administration for Children and Families, Administration on Children Youth and Families Children's Bureau; 2008. 1-194*
- http://emedicine.medscape.com/article/916007-overview(link is external)
- *http://www.americanhumane.org/(link is external)*
- *http://www.americanhumane.org/children/stop-child-abuse/fact-sheets/chil...(link is external)*
- *http://www.americanhumane.org/children/stop-child-abuse/fact-sheets/chil...(link is external)*
- *United States Department of Health and Human Services*
- *"Child Abuse and Neglect, Posttraumatic Stress Disorder(link is external)" by Angelo P Giardino, MD, PhD, Clinical Associate Professor, Department of Pediatrics, Baylor College of Medicine; Medical Director, Texas Children's Health Plan, Inc*
- *http://www.aacap.org*
- Jesch, Judith (2001). *Women in the Viking Age* (New ed.). Woodbridge, Suffolk: Boydell Press. p. 178. ISBN 9780851153605.

- Saxo Grammaticus (1979). Davidson, Hilda Ellis, ed. *The history of the Danes: books I-IX*. Translated by Fisher, Peter. Woodbridge: D. S. Brewer. p. 151. ISBN 9780859915021.
- Arthur Golden, *Memoirs of A Geisha*, (New York: Random House, 1997)ISBN 0-679-78158-7
- Paul Rhys Mountfort (2003), *Nordic Runes* (Rochester, Vermont: Destiny Books) ISBN 0-89281-093-9
- Lamsa, George, (Translator); Holy Bible: From the Ancient Eastern Test: George M. Lamsa's Translation From the Aramaic of the Peshitta. Harper & Row, 1985.
- https://billygraham.org/decision-magazine/january-2016/a-message-from-billy-graham-total-surrender/
- Letter To Mme. N. D. Fonvisin (1854), *Letters of Fyodor Michailovitch Dostoevsky to his Family and Friends* (1914), translated by Ethel Golburn Mayne, Letter XXI, p. 71
- Archbishop Luis M. Martinez, *True Devotion to the Holy Spirit* (Sophia Institute Press, 2000).
- MacArthur, John, Grace to You; Sermon Genesis 3:1-7; https://www.gty.org/library/sermons-library/90-234/the-breadth-and-depth-of-sin, Feb 6, 2000
- CS Lewis the Abolition of Man
- D'elbee, Father Jean C. J., I Believe in Love. Sophia Institute Press, New Hampshire, 2001
- Fr. Benedict J. Groeschel, C.F.R., Gerard and Yoland Cleffi, *Meditations from the Oratory, Experiencing the Mystery of Christ*, Our Sunday Visitor Publishing, 2008
- https://activechristianity.org/what-is-the-baptism-of-the-spirit
- Orlund Ph.D., Dane C., *ESV Expository Commentary: Romans – Galatians, Volume X*; Crossway, 2020
- CS Lewis, The Efficacy of Prayer, Fifteenth Printing, Forward Movement, 2003
- Fields, Rick, Chop Wood, Carry Water; Jeremy P, Tarcher/Putnam Books, New York, 1984
- Green, John, The Fault of Our Stars; Penguin Books, New York 2012
- Southey, Robert; The Fall of Robespierre. Play. 1794

- Pizzalato, Brian; Christ Gives Meaning to Suffering, article, Catholic News Agency
- Martinez, Archbishop Luis M., The Sanctifier. Pauline Books, 2003
- Stern, David H., *Complete Jew Bible: An English Version of he Tanakh(Old Testament) and B'rit Hadashah (New Testament.* Messianic Jewish Communications, 2011
- Lewis, C.S., The Problem of Pain. HarperCollins, New York, 1940.
- Harris, MD., M.D., *Daily Life in First Century Israel and the Roman Empire.* MD Harris Institute, 2011
- Beckwith, Francis, J., Natural Law, Catholicism, and the Protestant Critique: Why We Are Really Not That Far Apart. Christian Bioethics. Academic journal article. Academic.oup.com, 2019
- Aristotle (author), Bartlett, Robert C. (Translator), Collins, Susan D. (Translator); Aristotle's Nicomachean Ethics. University of Chicago Press, 2012.
- The Merriam-Webster Dictionary, Merriam-Webster, 2019

Printed in the United States
by Baker & Taylor Publisher Services